In & Out of
Paris

In & Out of ● Paris

Gardens of Secret Delights

ZAHID SARDAR / PHOTOGRAPHS BY MARION BRENNER

GIBBS SMITH
TO ENRICH AND INSPIRE HUMANKIND

First Edition

18 17 16 15 14   5 4 3 2 1

Published by
Gibbs Smith
P.O. Box 667
Layton, Utah 84041

1.800.835.4993 orders
www.gibbs-smith.com

Designed by Zahid Sardar Design
Printed and bound in China

Gibbs Smith books are printed on either recycled,
100% post-consumer waste, FSC-certified papers or
on paper produced from sustainable PEFC-certified
forest/controlled wood source.
Learn more at www.pefc.org.

Library of Congress Control Number: 2014937861
ISBN 13: 978-1-4236-3270-2

PAGES 2 AND 3: At the Tuileries Garden, a marble monument to
Charles Perrault, author of children's fables, by Gabriel Pech, and
The Tree of Vowels, a bronze sculpture by Giuseppe Penone.
PAGE 4: Monet's much-painted lily pond and bridge at Giverny.
PAGE 6: A resin door at Villa André Bloc in Meudon.
ABOVE: Suspended orchids by Jeff Leatham at the Hôtel George V.
FACING: Common snowberry (*Symphoricarpos albus* var. *laevigatus*).
OVERLEAF: Classical sculpture of a youth at the Palais Royal garden.

For our families

Contents

Introduction

Let us cultivate our garden.

— *Voltaire*

Outside the Walls

Paris, garden city

"A walk about Paris will provide lessons in history, beauty, and in the point of life," the statesman Thomas Jefferson said, bedazzled by the French capital in 1844, decades before Baron Haussmann, the prefect of Paris under Napoleon III, turned it into the verdant architectural marvel we know.

However, Jefferson would have seen the seeds of Paris's greening sown some three centuries earlier at Tuileries Palace, where Henry II's queen, Catherine de Medici, broke from Gothic traditions and encouraged a true absorption of Italian Renaissance garden ideals.

Her Tuileries Palace and Garden along the Seine were conceived in 1564, a few years after she abandoned the stultifying confines of medieval Paris, where her home, now replaced by Place des Vosges in the Marais, was the site of a celebratory joust that killed her husband. The widowed queen stood in for her three ineffectual sons, who were consecutive kings of France, first in the fortified Louvre outside the old city walls and then in a palace she built just west of it over a clay quarry where *tuiles,* or tiles, used to be made. Architect Philibert de L'Orme, who worked on chateaus outside Paris for the queen's archrival, Henry II's mistress, Diane de Poitiers, designed the palace. Seeking more civilized entertainment befitting absolute monarchs, de Medici commissioned an Italian, Bernard de Carnesse, to design something akin to the Florentine gardens of her youth. She wanted it to be the largest, most beautiful pleasure garden the city had ever known.

Francis I, de Medici's father-in-law and the engine of the French Renaissance, who had Italian artists such as Leonardo da Vinci in his retinue, had tried at his chateaus scattered in Blois, Chambord, and Fontainebleau to recreate gardens he had seen during expansionist campaigns in Italy, but the Tuileries Garden was not only more cohesive, it was truly Italian. More significantly, it fuelled one of the most important expansions of millennia-old Paris, which would then continue to grow in concentric rings around the city's ancient core.

PREVIOUS OVERLEAF: *The Tree of Vowels* by sculptor Giuseppe Penone. LEFT: Architect I. M. Pei's monumental 1989 glass and steel pyramid in the Louvre's Cour Napoleon echoes First Empire-period Egyptian-style iconography, as well as oblique references to the Holy Trinity and the Sun King, Louis XIV, in Catherine de Medici's 1564 Tuileries Garden (just beyond the green Jardin du Carrousel on the right edge) that was redesigned in 1664 by Le Nôtre.

The Tuileries sixteenth-century design went beyond the squared rigidity of monkish utilitarian herb gardens of lavender, marjoram, mint, and thyme. Its rectangular compartments, or parquets, divided by a grid of gravel-covered strolling paths, had sections decorated with the low-growing violets, lilies of the valley, primroses, peonies, irises, calendulas, snowdrops, and *Lilium candidum* of the medieval garden, as well as allegorical statues, fountains, a labyrinth, a grotto (an Italian Mannerist feature that became an essential and recurring motif in French gardens well into the nineteenth century) with colorful faience images of plants and animals, lawns, intimate groves of trees, kitchen gardens or potagers, and a vineyard. This all made for a joyful venue for cultured entertainment and lavish parties to rival those at de Medici's country chateau in Chenonceau.

Some years after de Medici's death in 1589, the 38-acre Tuileries Garden—which is nearly six times as large as the Louvre's Cour Napoleon, where architect I. M. Pei's 1989 glass pyramid now stands—was greatly altered by Henry IV and Marie de Medici, his Florentine queen who later became regent to a young Louis XIII and built herself the Luxembourg Palace and Gardens. Tuileries Palace, home to many monarchs after them, remained a work in progress until the nineteenth century, when it nearly closed off the U-shaped Louvre to form an interior courtyard. Shortly after that, the palace was torched and destroyed by rebels of the Paris Commune in 1871, the same year a defeated Napoleon III slipped into exile. However, many vestiges of the original Tuileries Garden remained intact alongside the garden's seventeenth-century additions.

The evolution and adaptation of the Tuileries both influenced and reflected garden trends in the Île-de-France, as the Seine Valley around Paris is called. The Tuileries was a garden to stroll in, but like other palatial gardens, French gardeners gradually redesigned it to be viewed from *piano nobile* windows and raised terraces.

FACING: Among many monuments at the Tuileries celebrating artists and writers, a marble bust by Gabriel Pech honors Charles Perrault, author of "Puss in Boots" and other children's tales.

TOP AND MIDDLE: The Jardin du Carrousel, reconfigured during the 1990s by Belgian designer Jacques Wirtz, has sand and stone paths, and yew hedges radiating from Napoleon's 1808 Arc de Triomphe du Carrousel. Sculptor Aristide Maillol's twentieth-century female bronzes "amble" amid Wirtz's hedges.

RIGHT: Le Nôtre's raised terrace, along the length of the park's south side, was—according to Pascal Cribier, who has been immersed in a decades-long restoration of the garden—imperceptibly lower in the middle to keep the Seine's messy edges out of view.

In time, its symmetrically arranged Italianate parquet enclosures on each side of a central axis were replaced by *parterres,* or planting beds "on the ground," that were decorated not just with flowers but also low, clipped dwarf box hedges that looked like the curvilinear arabesque patterns on woven Turkish carpets and embroidered silk brocades. These *parterres de broderie,* which brought sensuous curves and diagonals to rectilinear garden plans, were accented with brick dust, colored clay, and sand sprinkled between the boxwood so that they could be better viewed from a distance.

Parterres devised by Jacques Boyceau, superintendent of royal gardens under Louis XIII, and Jacques Mollet, who worked at de Poitiers' Chateau d'Anet, where

LEFT: Le Nôtre transformed the Italianate Tuileries Garden into a *jardin à la française* along the lines of Vaux-le-Vicomte, with symmetrical *parterres de broderie* separated by a long, wide processional walkway that had paths intersecting it at right angles. The Arc de Triomphe du Carrousel and the Louvre at the east end of the central axis can be seen from the Grand Bassin Rond pond, where Parisians can use one of the 3,000 green chairs supplied. BELOW: The center of the park is where designers Pascal Cribier and Louis Benech planted a profusion of colorful flowering perennials that allude to richly costumed nobles who once strolled there.

Italian formal gardening was first introduced, were later mastered by Mollet's son, Claude Mollet, the royal gardener for Henry IV, Louis XIII, and Louis XIV, and "embroidered" *parterres* edged with boxwood like those at the Tuileries became the essence of French formal gardens. They were the carpets of outdoor rooms that began to be more clearly defined. Ornamental architectural trellises and arbors of wood for shade evolved into canopies of stone, and groves of trees were clipped into green walls to form *cabinets de verdure* and *bosquets*. Flowers, once so loved, were now grown as demure borders or in separate *parterres de fleurs* and *parterres* of cutwork. They played a lesser role at the Tuileries, where hedges were designed to be beautiful in every season, and in gardens where ponds reflected architecture and water coursed prominently through canals and from fountains.

The Tuileries Garden, adjacent to the reins of power, became the disseminator of this growing French style as well as the cradle of France's most famous *paysagiste,* or landscape architect. André Le Nôtre, whose forbears tended the Tuileries and also worked under the Mollets, learned his craft at his parent's home within the Tuileries Garden. At the Palais du Louvre's academy of the arts next door, he learned about painting, perspective, mathematics, and architecture, and also

cultivated crucial friendships with painter Charles le Brun and architect François Mansart. Le Nôtre and le Brun went on to dazzle the French with a garden for Nicolas Fouquet, Louis XIV's minister of finance. Uniquely, their new garden, which had subsumed the land of three whole villages, shared a central axis with Fouquet's chateau by architect Louis Le Vau, and the two elements formed a unitary, indivisible whole. Such a concept was not unknown in Italy, where the lines of a villa were often aligned to a garden, but Le Nôtre's version of a well-ordered, symmetrical axial garden had less-obvious perspectives, unique optical illusions, and hidden alcoves and surprises that exceeded any Italian original. It proved seminal and became the template for

FACING, TOP: Near Sacré-Coeur Basilica, Clos Montmartre is a unique public garden. Planted in 1933 on a small hillside, it is Paris's last remaining winery, with 2,000 vines that produce wines that are auctioned annually—with labels designed by artists—during the Fête des Vendanges funded by the Mairie de Montmartre.
RIGHT: Near Les Halles Park, retaining walls for the Métro's *bouche* become a hanging garden. Above it are the Paris Bourse de Commerce and the 90-foot column of Catherine de Medici from 1575.
FACING, BOTTOM, AND BELOW: More views of *The Tree of Vowels*. The bronze sculpture by Giuseppe Penone is an eloquent reminder of 1990s storms that prompted restoration work at the Tuileries.

the Sun King Louis XIV's larger and more elaborate Versailles and countless other Le Nôtre gardens, where optical effects achieved with mathematical precision made gardens appear longer, boundaries disappear, and gentle slopes vanish into the horizon. No longer Italian, this was the *jardin à la française* now.

Versailles' forested swamps (where water, a critical element for such grand gardens, was always in short supply) were turned, with the aid of pumps and hydraulics, into a fountain-filled wonderland for Louis XIV's permanent court, where visiting monarchs could watch mock naval battles in a vast double cruciform canal or in water *parterres* possibly inspired by Renaissance water gardens like Courances.

Techniques developed at Versailles were redeployed in many royal gardens, and between 1667 and 1671, Le Nôtre returned home to the Tuileries to add a wider central promenade that formed the basis for Paris's Axe Historique that now extends from the Louvre, through the Champs-Élysées, past Napoleon's Arc de Triomphe, and westward to the modern-day arch of La Défense. On the south side of the garden he installed a *grande terrasse du bord de l'eau* that is still both a promenade along the Seine as well as a low wall to protect the garden. Three round basins close to the palace—alluding to notions of the Sun King's self-proclaimed divinity—and a giant octagonal pond at the west end also remain. The Tuileries, subtly restored and modernized during the last two decades by landscape architects Pascal Cribier and Louis Benech, once again reflects the symmetry and the regal promenade Le Nôtre installed during the *grand siècle*.

FACING: The 61-acre Parc des Buttes Chaumont in the 19th arrondissement, where lovers have been trysting since 1867, was unveiled during the second Paris Universal Exposition by Jean-Charles Alphand, who, under the aegis of Napoleon III, created most of Paris's major parks. The former gypsum quarry's *Anglo-Chinois* design incorporates architect Gabriel Davioud's Italianate Temple de la Sibylle, which hovers 150 feet above an artificial lake.

TOP, RIGHT: In 1985, architects Bernard Tschumi and Colin Fournier converted a 19th arrondissement site for slaughterhouses into Parc de la Villette, a deconstructivist science and industry park where people can also relax. La Géode, a shining stainless steel geodesic dome by architect Adrien Fainsilber, contains an IMAX theater.

MIDDLE: *Parterres*, garden paths, and *allées* are reimagined in Parc de la Villete's ten minimalist or fantastically themed gardens.

RIGHT: Marie de Medici's 1611 Jardin du Luxembourg's Fountain of the Observatory, also called the Carpeaux Fountain because its principal sculptures are by Jean-Baptiste Carpeaux, came after the elegant Avenue de l'Observatoire by Gabriel Davioud in 1867.

However, the *jardin à la française* favored by Louis XIV as an emblem of absolute monarchy that could even bend nature to his will lost considerable steam after the king's death in 1715. Increasingly powerful nobles in the weakened courts of Louis XV and Louis XVI acquired *hôtels particuliers* and townhouses in Paris or returned to their neglected country estates away from Versailles, where those who had been exposed to London favored picturesque English landscape gardens over the formal baroque French garden.

Explorers, colonists, and landscape artists such as Hubert Robert stoked a new fascination for exotic gardens and a hybridized French landscape garden tradition, which emerged in the mid-eighteenth century. Designers melded the *jardin à la française* with meandering English landscapes laced with Asian aesthetics. Exotic Chinese and Japanese pagodas, English-style Gothic ruins, classical temples, windmills, and even mock farms were incorporated into French gardens.

Marquis René de Girardin, author of *De la composition des paysages,* was among the first proponents of the *jardin Anglo-Chinois,* as they came to be called. At his Ermenonville garden 25 miles northeast of Paris, a Temple of Philosophy was dedicated to his mentor Jean-Jacques Rousseau, who advocated a return to nature and the "simple life." The style's most avant-garde example, the Désert de Retz, was popular among nobles

who slipped away from the stilted atmosphere of Louis XVI's Versailles, across the forest of Marly, and through a grotto entrance to enjoy the hedonistic, magical "deserted" setting provided by aristocrat François Racine de Monville. Soon, Marie Antoinette's Hameau de la Reine at Versailles and other examples of this kind of French landscape garden popped up rapidly, one after the other, like bubbles in a flute of champagne.

The French Revolution—ironically fueled by some of the very egalitarian ideas Rousseau proffered—stopped such horticultural and arboreal extravagance in its tracks. But the French landscape aesthetic weathered the doldrums of the post-Revolution regimes and the Napoleonic decade of the early nineteenth century, before it resurfaced during and after Napoleon III's Second Empire, alongside Monet's Impressionism and Rodin's Modernism. It was no surprise. The last formal gardens looked codified and static, and with scarcer resources for keeping them clipped, people readily reverted to pastoral landscapes and flowers.

In 1853, Haussmann began the incredible transformation of Paris, reconfiguring the city into 20 manageable *arrondissements,* all linked with grand, gas-lit boulevards and new arteries of running water to feed large public parks and beautiful gardens influenced greatly by London's Kew Gardens. In every quarter, the indefatigable prefect, in concert with engineer Jean-Charles Alphand, refurbished neglected estates such as Parc Monceau and the Jardin du Luxembourg, and transformed royal hunting enclaves into new parks such as enormous Bois de Boulogne and Bois de Vincennes. They added romantic Parc des Buttes Chaumont and Parc Montsouris in areas that were formerly inhospitable quarries, as well as dozens of smaller neighborhood gardens that Alphand described as "green and flowering salons."

Thanks to hothouses that sprang up in Paris, inspired by England's prefabricated cast iron and glass factory buildings and huge exhibition halls such as the Crystal Palace, exotic blooms became readily available for small

Parisian gardens. For example, nineteenth-century metal and glass conservatories added by Charles Rohault de Fleury to the Jardin des Plantes, Louis XIII's 1626 royal botanical garden for medicinal plants, provided ideal conditions for orchids, tulips, and other plant species from around the globe. Other steel structures, such as Victor Baltard's 12 metal and glass market stalls at Les Halles in the 1850s, also heralded the coming of Paris's most enduring symbol, Gustave Eiffel's 1889 Universal Exposition tower, and the installation of steel viaducts for trains to all parts of France. Word of this new Paris brought about emulative City Beautiful movements in most European capitals, and in the United States, Bois de Boulogne and Parc des Buttes Chaumont became models for Frederick Law Olmsted's Central Park in New York.

Meanwhile, for Parisians fascinated by the lakes, cascades, grottoes, lawns, flowerbeds, and trees that transformed their city from just another ancient capital into a lyrical, magical garden city, the new Paris became a textbook for cross-pollinating garden ideas at any scale. Royal gardens and exotic public pleasure grounds of the Second Empire became springboards for gardens such as Bernard Tschumi's vast, conceptual Parc de La Villette, with its modern follies, and "wild" *jardins en mouvement* at the Fondation Cartier and the Musée du Quai Branly. In turn, *allées* of trees in some classic formal gardens were allowed to grow freely or were interleaved with wildflower meadows and wild grasses for their unsung beauty. Private gardens hidden behind *hôtel particulier* walls, gardens in spacious suburbs, city courtyards, and minuscule rooftop terraces, became expressions of old and very new gardens that synthesized nature, art, and outdoors living.

In these pages, the largest historic gardens, and some new ones grouped as estates or public gardens, provide contextual backdrops for Parisian designs as diverse as botanist Patrick Blanc's *mur vegetals,* Pierre Bergé's artful retreat, florist Jeff Leatham's installations, follies by artist André Bloc, a terrace gallery by artist MariCarmen Hernandez, a Japanese garden for fashion designer Kenzo Takada, an intimate rooftop enclave by couturier Martin Grant, another by artist Jean-Michel Othoniel, gardens by landscape architects Cribier, Benech, Gilles Clément, Camille Muller, Hugues Peuvergne, Pierre-Alexandre Risser, and Christian Fournet, and a few more by the architectural firms Agence Jouin Manku, Jakob + MacFarlane, and Ateliers Michael Herrman.

Their stories will hopefully, as Paris did Jefferson, surprise you and "provide lessons in history, beauty, and in the point of life."

FACING TOP: At the three-acre Jardin de l'Intendant, the Garden of the Steward, on the southwest corner of the vast parade grounds of Hôtel des Invalides in Paris, salvias, grasses, and fragrant fennel (*Foeniculum vulgare*) contrast with the four-foot-high conical clipped yew topiaries and parterres in the formal garden based on eighteenth-century designs. Low boxwood cutwork parterres filled with flowers are retrieving lost ground in the *jardin à la française.*
FACING, LEFT: At Courances, which predates Le Nôtre's Vaux-le-Vicomte, stands of unclipped plane trees and wildflower meadows again take the place of formal lawns and strictly clipped allées.

Garden Estates

A garden to walk in and immensity to dream in . . .
what more could he ask? A few flowers at his feet and
above him the stars.
— *Victor Hugo*

Inspired Vaux-le-Vicomte

The garden that launched the Louis XIV style

It took just one 100-acre *grand siècle* garden to launch one of France's most celebrated landscape architects and write the grammar of French formal gardens for the next hundred years.

In 1656, Viscount Nicolas Fouquet, King Louis XIV's minister of finance, began building his baroque chateau and a garden within a 1,200-acre estate in Maincy, an hour south of Paris. In plan and aesthetics the Chateau de Vaux-le-Vicomte and its garden were indeed unprecedented, but they became so widely influential only through a quirk of history.

The raised stone chateau surrounded by a moat and ancillary brick buildings, designed by architect Louis Le Vau, were linked to the lively geometry of a mile-long, rectangular garden by landscape architect André Le Nôtre. Because the unified design was unveiled during a fete honoring Louis XIV in 1660, the relatively

PREVIOUS OVERLEAF: *Parterres de broderie* seen from the Chateau de Vaux-le-Vicomte. A grotto and statue of Hercules in the distance.
LEFT: The domed chateau seen from the grand Canal de la Poêle.
BELOW: Leonine sculptures and ponds mirror "untamed" nature.
OVERLEAF: The façade seen from the *parterre de fleurs* by Louis Benech.

unknown duo, working for the first time at this scale alongside painter Charles le Brun, also prepared rooms for the visiting monarch, never anticipating that their lavishness would arouse envy and suspicion. The king accused his minister of embezzling state coffers to build Vaux, then imprisoned him and commandeered the designers to build an even grander spectacle at his family's country estate in Versailles.

The royal retreat went from being a hunting park to a dazzling symbol of power modeled after Vaux, and such *jardins à la française* became the lingua franca of palace gardens everywhere.

After Fouquet's imprisonment, Vaux-le-Vicomte was neglected and would have been demolished had not Alfred Sommier, a wealthy sugar baron, rescued it in 1875. Thanks to original engravings of the garden, Vaux's simple plan, its monumental scale and gloriously varied details could be revived. Sommier's descendants, including Patrice and Cristina de Vogüé, the comte and comtesse de Vogüé, now own and manage the estate with their three sons.

LEFT: The *cour d'honneur,* or entry court, seen from the raised chateau.
BELOW: Chateau lawns accented by hedges and conical topiaries.
OVERLEAF: The silhouetted *Farnese Hercules* above the Canal de la Poêle's *grottes,* which are not visible until walkers come upon them.

"We view ourselves as custodians of Le Nôtre's vision," eldest son Alexandre de Vogüé said.

Vaux's chateau and garden were linked by their central visual axis—which came to characterize the much-imitated "Louis XIV" style, favoring lengthy vistas and panoramic swoops across the landscape that were modulated by symmetrical lawns, gravel paths, classical statuary and topiaries. Le Nôtre, a trained architect, used forced perspectives and varied heights and shapes to compose a landscape that could be seen at a glance, but his genius lay in providing surprises up close. Opposite the chateau's south façade, two identical *parterres de broderie* composed of clipped hedges, like the English knot gardens sixteenth-century gardener Claude Mollet made popular, were laid out like arabesque carpets to be viewed from up high, but hidden grottoes on the sides could be seen only while walking in the garden. Oblique paths opened up unexpected views of fountains and reflecting ponds, and distant woods blurred the limits of the garden and shaded walkways bordering a lawn up the farthest hill. The river Anqueil flowing through

the garden was canalized to form the Canal de la Poêle, with *grottes,* or massive retaining walls, inset with seven rocaille niches on one side and cascades on the other, all so skillfully integrated below eye level that they seemed invisible until the moment of discovery.

Across the canal, a balustraded overlook atop the *grottes* offered reverse views of the garden, and on the hill above it a copy of the colossal *Farnese Hercules* stood against the sky. The muscled figure from the Baths of Caracalla belonged to Rome's papal Farneses, and Le Nôtre picked it as a symbol of Fouquet's power.

The statue was the climax to the suite of gardens and water basins extending from the chateau where le Brun had painted scenes from the complicated life of Hercules. Given what happened between Fouquet and Louis XIV, the Sun King, the designers were prescient, because, as the myth goes, even mighty Hercules was just a pawn of chance.

FACING: Seen through an *allée* of chestnut trees, an 1891 gilded lead copy of the *Farnese Hercules* replaced one Le Nôtre installed.
BELOW: More statuary and ponds within groves off the central axis.

Magnificent Versailles

André Le Nôtre's garden for the senses

"Such symmetry," nineteenth-century poet Lord Byron observed in Louis XIV's enviable gardens at the Chateau de Versailles, "is not for solitude." Designed for pleasure, the baroque gardens represent the zenith of the *jardin à la française,* with long sight lines and breathtaking details.

After 1661, landscape architect André Le Nôtre, architect Louis Le Vau and sculptor Charles le Brun transformed Louis XIII's former hunting lodge into a palace, and 2,000 acres of farmland and woods to its west became a stirring display of fountains and structural effects for the king's entertainment. Circular ponds, *parterres* with flowers and arabesque boxwood hedges, conical topiaries and statuary in the tiered garden all outshone any they created for the king's hapless minister at Vaux-le-Vicomte.

The sun, Louis XIV's emblem of royal divinity, was the underlying conceit. Radiating gravel paths, symbolizing rays of light, broke the garden's axial cross plan centered on a palace that was the epitome of French power.

LEFT AND BELOW: The Pièce d'Eau des Suisses lake dug by Swiss Guard regiments near Jules Hardouin-Mansart's 1684 arabesque Orangerie. Nearly 50 full-time gardeners maintain Versailles' gardens. OVERLEAF: At the crossroads of several groves, a gilded lead fountain by Jean-Baptiste Tuby honors Flora, goddess of flowers and spring.

Le Nôtre, a trained architect aware of the effects of foreshortening, made the mile-long Grand Canal for boating parties on the east–west axis seem like a wide pool of light, and a shorter polygonal *tapis vert*, or lawn for the king to walk on, a matching pool of green. Between the two, he placed a fountain designed by le Brun that depicts Apollo, the sun god, riding his golden chariot.

Le Vau's nod to the sun—the Orangerie on a slope at the chateau's south end—was later enlarged by Jules Hardouin-Mansart to accommodate more potted citrus trees and *parterres*. He continued to enhance other elements in Le Nôtre's unfolding masterpiece, and a large reservoir called Pièce d'Eau des Suisses, excavated by the king's Swiss Guard in 1678 from 40 acres of marshland near the Orangerie, was also a place for naval exercises.

However, Le Nôtre's squared *bosquets,* or groves, containing grottoes and fantastic tiered theaters with sculptural fountains, cascades and vertical jets, all framed by *palissades*—the labor-intensive clipped yew hedging that formed towering walls—are among his key triumphs. Few of these outdoor salons, where fêtes lasted for days, fully survived storms and changing fashions that uprooted plantings with equal vengeance. Nonetheless, water—Versailles' star element—still courses down to groves and fountains from a reservoir at the north end of the palace, through a network of pipes that drains into the Grand Canal situated on lower ground, and is recirculated via wind-powered hydraulic pumps. Restored *bosquets* continue to delight thousands, who come to enjoy Versailles' gardens as their own since the French Revolution.

The groves sometimes serve as a museum for nature-inspired sculptors such as Giuseppe Penone, and in the 350-year-old Théâtre d'Eau, or Water Theater, grove that was radically altered by Louis XVI and then obliterated by a storm in 1999, modern art finally has a permanent corner. Reinterpreted with new plantings and water basins by landscape designer Louis Benech in 2014, this grove sports sculptor Jean-Michel Othoniel's four blown-glass fountains, whose delicate arabesque shapes allude, aptly, to patterns Louis XIV might have traced while dancing a minuet.

PREVIOUS OVERLEAF: The 1675 Bosquet de l'Encelade fountain by Gaspard Marsy depicting Enceladus, a dying Titan under the rocks of Mt. Olympus, is an allegory for Louis XIV's victory over insurgents.
FACING: *Elevazione,* an arboreal sculpture by artist Giuseppe Penone shown during the 400th-anniversary celebrations of Le Nôtre's birth in the Bosquet de l'Étoile, echoes Enceladus's struggle.
RIGHT, TOP: Classic conical topiaries and statues along the walkways.
RIGHT: Boxwood cutwork *parterres* infilled again with flowers.
OVERLEAF: The Bassin d'Apollon fountain, sculpted by Jean-Baptiste Tuby.

Reflections at Courances

A Renaissance water garden

Courances, whose mellifluous name alludes to running water, has been a princely estate since the Middle Ages, and it reflects several centuries of French garden styles, all linked by water.

That's because, like Venice or Amsterdam, Courances, in the marshy plain of the river École, 30 miles south of Paris, virtually floats on it.

Although there are few extant records of the garden, it is believed that its ingenious canals, built to tame springs as well as the river on its western edge, date back to the sixteenth century. The waters still flow, somewhat eccentrically, from one canal to another and, eventually, through culverts into the river. Alongside the École, a quarter-mile-long Grand Canal, bordered today by unclipped *allées* of poplars, easily predates other gargantuan canals like it.

Located on the western edge of the vast Corot-esque Fontainebleau Forest, Courances was also the coveted source for clear drinking water for Fontainebleau Palace, where the royal families of France took up residence.

In keeping with such elite neighbors, Claude Gallard, Courances's seventeenth-century owner, built a Louis XIII–style chateau in 1622 with pyramidal slate roofs and tall brick chimneys, and, rumor had it, his heirs also invited the celebrated landscape architect André Le Nôtre to create a *parc à la française* replete with an axial plan, a moat encircling the building and a wide entry courtyard with a central carriageway on the north side flanked by canals. These additions, whether they were Le Nôtre's or those of an acolyte, helped to establish the semblance of a symmetrical plan.

To accent and reflect the verdant setting, nearly 14 springs were also channeled into more than a dozen ornamental ponds. Designed by others, Le Miroir, a two-acre lake on the southern axis of the 185-acre garden, may have inspired Le Nôtre's version at Vaux-le-Vicomte.

Unlike undulating Vaux-le-Vicomte, Courances is flat and so "walls" of oak, lime, yew and horse chestnut trees planted in rows and hornbeam *palissades* of different heights brought variation. Wolf and lion sculptures and sentinel statues atop pedestals placed between tall hedges bordered a green walkway alongside Les Nappes, the sixteenth-century three-tiered cascade engineered to flow smoothly from level to level, propelled solely by gravity toward the diagonal Grand Canal.

In 1768, the Salle d'Eau, a rectangular pond west of the chateau with gargoyle-shaped water spouts, was reshaped as an ornamental lake, and around the same time, Anne-Catherine Gallard opened up the north wall and entryway to form a true *cour d'honneur* with twin *allées* of lime trees that have since been replaced by plane trees.

The influence of picturesque English-style gardens became increasingly stronger at Courances after 1772 when the edges of more of its ponds were blurred in the interest of naturalism.

The gardeners need not have tried so hard. After the French Revolution, the property was abandoned for nearly 40 years and a horse chestnut evidently grew through the floors of the chateau.

FACING: Boxwood *parterres de broderie* on the south side of the Chateau de Courances. Roses and hydrangeas are espaliered in an asymmetrical composition against the chateau walls.
BELOW: A stone lion rests beside Les Nappes canals and wild, untrimmed *allées* of plane trees are boxed in by neat hedges.
OVERLEAF: A carefully trimmed architectural *palissade* gateway to the Anglo-Japanese garden is a stellar example of French garden craft.

German banker Baron Samuel de Haber came to the rescue in 1872 and began Courances's rejuvenation. He and his son-in-law, Count Octave de Béhague, enlisted architect Gabriel-Hippolyte Destailleur to restore the overgrown garden's ponds and channels and bring back the Renaissance-era chateau with a new skin of rosy brick and white sandstone.

The sludge dredged from canals filled unnecessary channels and the moat on the south side, while the rest of the garden was landscaped with gravel paths, new turf and statuary. Destailleur did not entirely ignore the formal axis of the garden, and between the chateau and its mirror lake he added a pond with a dolphin fountain.

Henri and Achille Duchêne, a father and son landscape architecture team, who revived many dilapidated estates including Blenheim—England's answer to Versailles—as well as Vaux-le-Vicomte early in the twentieth century, were also responsible for Courances's rebirth.

ABOVE: The Anglo-Japanese garden around the old mill pond with an island, a weeping willow and Japanese maple in the middle.
LEFT: La Foulerie teahouse opens to the Anglo-Japanese garden.
FACING: An unlined canal near a gateway building feeds the moat.
OVERLEAF: *Allées* of untrimmed plane trees beside the canals of the *cour d'honneur* entryway to the chateau.

Working in concert with Courances's Marquis Jean de Ganay and his wife, the Marquise Berthe de Béhague, Baron de Haber's granddaughter, the Duchênes reestablished the formal garden in novel ways. Long, straight canals were set in curbs of stone on either side of the central stretch of lawn, and rows of trees, planted to converge in the distance, forced the perspective and made vistas looking south seem longer than they were. They added twin *parterres de broderie* of boxwood in arabesque patterns interspersed with colored gravel very like those at Vaux-le-Vicomte, and unified old and new sections of the garden by using the sandstone gargoyle water spouts from the original Salle d'Eau in as many canals as possible. At the head of a new horseshoe-shaped pool on the east side, they created the Fountain of Aréthuse, topped with a marble nymph sculpted by Claude Poirier in 1711 for the royal grounds of Marly.

In 1908, east of the chateau, next to a rustic teahouse called La Foulerie that used to be an old sawmill, Berthe de Béhague, the Marquise de Ganay, decided to add an Anglo-Japanese garden where naturalized bulbs, Judas tree blossoms, foxgloves, herbaceous geraniums, peonies and maple leaves add seasonal color. Kathleen Lloyd Jones, an English protégé of Gertrude Jekyll, the inventor of mixed borders in the English garden, came to lend a hand in this asymmetrical creation.

During World War II when German and, subsequently, American troops occupied the chateau, the gardens suffered gravely. A young Jean-Louis de Ganay, trained in agriculture, returned from the war to the rescue. Practical and modern, he decided to leave the *allées* unclipped, and allowed meadows to form over lawns and made more room for a more romantic garden. He planted poplars along the Grand Canal, and the Japanese garden became the domain of his wife, Philippine de Ganay.

The next generation, led by their daughter Valentine Hansen de Ganay, a writer, continues to modify the private park that also sports a nearby potager for the public.

Hansen de Ganay, who keeps an apartment under the eaves at Courances and a rooftop terrace in Paris, wistfully describes the garden as "a kind of miracle," perhaps because despite its tumultuous history, the murmur of its waters goes on.

FACING: A picturesque English-style corner of Courances with a square stone fountain within one of its many pools.
RIGHT, TOP: A replica of the nymph atop the Fountain of Aréthuse. The original 1711 marble by Claude Poirier is at the Louvre.
RIGHT: The Salle d'Eau gargoyles reinstalled by the Duchênes in stone-lined pools. In the background, the horseshoe pool and the white Fountain of Aréthuse at its head.

Rodin's Sculpture Garden

A gallery of light, and hidden spaces

"Nature and Antiquity are the two great sources of life for an artist," the nineteenth-century sculptor Auguste Rodin once said, and at his studio in the Hôtel Biron, an elegant 1730s rococo mansion near Les Invalides, he surrounded himself with both. The estate, open to the public since 1919 as the Musée Rodin, once belonged to the horticulturist Maréchal de Biron. It has one of Paris's most visited gardens, where Rodin's seminal modern work, which was inspired ironically by classic Greek and Roman torsos, is displayed.

The Burghers of Calais, the infamous statue of Honoré de Balzac, *The Thinker*, *Orpheus Imploring the Gods*, *The Three Shades*, and nearly 1,000 other lesser-known Rodin works in plaster, bronze and marble are shown either in the mansion or outdoors.

The seven-and-a-half-acre walled garden, originally designed for wealthy financier Abraham Peyrenc de Moras by Jean Aubert, was essentially a country estate replete with a potager. It now comprises a front rose garden, and a south terrace and formal rectangular garden behind the mansion. The south garden culminates in a circular pond and a 20-foot-tall hornbeam hedge supported by a trellis with three arched openings that conceals a secluded picnic spot at the end.

The garden's evolution echoes the estate's history. When de Biron acquired the property from de Moras's widow during the late eighteenth century, he altered its formal plantings to make room for the circular pool and English-style beds that are well documented in engravings. The gardens on each side of the house were either altered or neglected over the centuries as the home was sometimes rented by the day or used as a papal residence, a consulate, a nunnery, a boarding school for girls and finally, when it was in the hands of the state, leased to artists including writer Jean Cocteau, painter Henri Matisse, dancer Isadora Duncan and sculptor, and future wife of poet Rainer Maria Rilke, Clara Westhoff, who invited Rodin into the enclave in 1908. Although the once stately gardens had become part orchard and pastureland, they appealed to Rodin, who could see

LEFT, TOP: Clipped and less-manicured plants amidst the lush rockery in the Garden of Orpheus in the eastern section of the garden.
LEFT: *The Three Shades,* a composition in bronze that was later incorporated into Rodin's *Gates of Hell,* which is in the rose garden.
FACING: Rodin's unusual monument to Balzac was posthumously cast.

them from his studio in the Hôtel Biron's lower south-facing rooms. Rodin enjoyed the naturalistic profusion of the ornamental garden enlarged by de Biron and was inspired to add his collection of antiques and his most avant-garde works to the contained wilderness, not as decoration but as living forms.

Rodin eventually convinced the French government to allow him exclusive use of the estate, paying the rent with his works, until his death in 1917. After he died, the house became a museum for the collection he left the nation.

Restored and tamed, the Rodin garden continues as an outdoor gallery. Some bronzes stand exactly where Rodin placed them before World War I, and conservators carefully preserve their patina. The eastern section of the garden invites walkers to explore plants and sculpture amid a shaded rockery that forms the Garden of Orpheus, and on the west side, water features quintessentially define the pollarded Garden of Springs.

LEFT: Looking west from the Garden of Springs, the rich dome of Les Invalides designed by Jules Hardouin-Mansart rises above trees.
BELOW: South of Hôtel Biron, a large ornamental garden has a hornbeam hedge backed by a trellis with arched openings that cordons off a quiet area with chaises to rest on.

Désert de Retz Follies

An *Anglo-Chinois* foil for formal French gardens

Fifteen miles west of central Paris, François Nicolas Henri Racine de Monville, an aristocratic eighteenth-century bon vivant and former grand master of waters and forests of Normandy, built 20 very exotic follies, or *fabriques,* that included real and false ruins on a hundred acres beside the royal Forêt de Marly near Chambourcy. However, Désert de Retz, his picturesque, Romantic, English-style *parc à fabriques* built from 1774 to 1789 to evoke an ephemeral past, was soon made literally desolate by French revolutionaries. History, time and neglect conspired to destroy this Eden of ornamental plants and trees, a potager and a dairy farm, yet they spared 10 follies, including the pyramidal Icehouse, the Roman Temple of Pan and the Colonne Détruite, a gigantic truncated 55-foot-high, 50-foot-wide Doric stone column that cleverly envelops Monville's four-story summer retreat and a skylit spiral staircase within it.

Long after its last noted occupant, Nobel laureate Frédéric Passy, died in 1912, preservationists began to restore the standing structures as well as nurse back an American redwood, trees from Africa and China, a centuries-old marcotted lime tree and assorted sycamore, chestnut, linden and ash trees. Only a small section of Monville's visionary garden survives, but its reputation as a naturalistic utopia that inspired Marie Antoinette, Swedish King Gustav III, Thomas Jefferson, and surrealists Dali and André Breton, looms large.

LEFT: The Temple of Pan and the white multistory Colonne Détruite.
BELOW: The restored pyramidal Icehouse is another valiant survivor.

Monet's Colorful Giverny

A painter's box of seasonal surprises

When artist Claude Monet painted his gardens, on two and a half acres sloping down from his pink crushed-brick farmhouse in Normandy's pastoral Giverny, just 50 miles west of Paris, he brought the world's gaze to them.

During the 1890s, the famous Impressionist converted a rectangular cider orchard with a central *allée* into a large garden of gridded gravel pathways, roses and clematis climbing up green-painted iron archways, colorful shrubs and an unrestrained painterly mix of exotic bulbs and flowers in beds. Then, just across the road from this walled "Clos Normand," Monet established an asymmetrical water garden that is fed by the Epte, a tributary of the Seine. Its large water lily pond, green footbridge, wisterias, weeping willows and azaleas, all inspired by Japanese engravings in his collection, are among the most recognizable subjects ever painted. And yet, because both gardens, linked together by a tunnel, offer unexpected, colorful blossoms each

LEFT, BELOW AND OVERLEAF: Monet controlled colors in his garden as he did paint on canvas. When a petal was soiled by soot, it was wiped clean. Irises, peonies, poppies, geraniums, delphiniums, azaleas and roses run amok in the Clos Normand outside his home.

season, they continue to inspire others who see them.

It is as if the artist still roams the restored estate that is now run as a museum under the auspices of the Fondation Claude Monet. Flowerbeds have clumps of Asian peonies, long-stemmed hollyhocks and colorful annuals, and fruit as well as ornamental trees create a backdrop for roses. Purple summer blooms, common daisies and poppies blend in with rare botanical specimens like those Monet often acquired from friends as well traveled as he. Nasturtiums flood the central *allée* of the clos, and by the pond, mauve dame's rockets (*Hesperis matronalis*), rhododendrons, blue lupines, pink sweet williams, white foxgloves and blue sages thrive alongside a bamboo wood and the famous nymphaea water lilies Monet liked to paint every summer.

The gardens, posed like still lifes in a "studio" outdoors where the artist walked or rowed in his boat, soon became an excuse to translate mists and water reflections into paint. Hundreds of Monet's paintings—small details blown up on wall-sized canvases with broad brushstrokes—became the genesis of modern abstract art, but "my garden is my most beautiful masterpiece," he always said.

LEFT AND ABOVE: Monet's famous Japanese footbridge was hand-made by peasant craftsmen in Giverny and rebuilt of beechwood when it finally succumbed to the weight of wisteria and rot. It is as iconic as the nymphaea water lilies, bamboo groves and weeping willows, also immortalized in paint.

Experimental Parc Méry-sur-Oise

Pascal Cribier's abandoned ode to water

"Gardens and landscapes are complementary but they are separate things and require different approaches," Pascal Cribier said, convinced that landscape architecture has to be functional while gardens can afford to be decorative, emotional "reductions" of natural landscapes. Yet Cribier, the principal landscape architect of the 1990s restoration of Le Nôtre's Tuileries Garden in Paris, created a botanical park 15 miles north of the capital that blurs the line between the two.

In 1999, in collaboration with botanist Patrick Blanc and architect Lionel Guibert, he transformed the 66-acre Seine Valley estate surrounding the historic Renaissance-era Chateau de Méry-sur-Oise, which belonged to Vivendi (an international media conglomerate that began as a waterworks company known as Compagnie Générale des Eaux), into an experimental, didactic water park.

In front of the chateau, the trio added two asymmetrical rectangular lakes—one for clear water and the other for a supply of brackish water—that echoed *parterres* that once existed there in a classic Le Nôtre-style *jardin à la française*. Cribier also introduced wild grasses, planted in decorative bands along an existing nineteenth-

LEFT: Next to a bamboo thicket, *Euonymus fortunei* 'Sarcoxie' vines growing on steel armatures form an *allée* of "topiaries."
BELOW: Circular concrete basins for estuarine plants and catalpa pom-poms grafted onto artificially extended trunks survived.

century promenade and a meandering English-style "river" attributed to Napoleon's landscape architect, Louis-Martin Berthault, and to Louis-Sulpice Varé, creator of Paris's Bois de Boulogne.

Cribier's most significant intervention besides the majestic water *parterres* was a garden on the eastern end of the estate where misty, hot, cold, brackish and mineralized water in the form of rain or waterfalls reigned. Comprising three thematic groves—La Dynamique, La Mineralisation and La Thermique—the garden was a place for observing the effects on plants of precipitation, salinization and temperatures ranging from tropical to arctic. In one section, a wide range of flora was exposed to torrents of recycled water gushing from overhead pipes. In another, exotic plants lived off mists, and in yet another area they derived sustenance from minerals and salts leached into the soil.

"Thanks to the qualities of specific types of water," plants adapted and even morphed differently than they do in nature, Cribier observed. In this sense, each discrete grove, linked by forested, shaded or barely covered walkways to the others, was a unique landscape to study the adaptability of plants outside their own ecosystems.

However, neglected since 2003, when Vivendi foundered financially and stopped irrigation, the cylindrical concrete troughs, raised rectangular beds, vaulted pipe canopies, and freestanding, 15-foot-high volcanic rock–filled gabion walls with a network of pipes for misting, spraying, flooding or drenching plants growing in or on the walls, have all been defunct. They remain standing, eerily beautiful like follies in *Anglo-Chinois* gardens.

Native and exotic plants, as well as hybridized catalpa balls growing on artificially elongated trunks that survived, are all part of a truly mutant garden where the edges of groves, custom concrete pavers laid in neat strips for walkways and beaten jungle paths are all blurred under thistles, hawkweed and grasses. The team's experimental "follies" have also been colonized by nature, and fireweed and yellow scabious sprout in areas previously meant for estuarine plants whose supply of water, minerals and salts is long gone.

Nonetheless, with its essential armature intact for more than a decade, the once-verdant otherworldly park could be revived, and that is something the town of Méry-sur-Oise, which oversees the estate, intends. Until that happens, Cribier revels in its sleeping beauty as if this poetic garden is what he planned all along.

FACING AND RIGHT: Erect and tilted gabion walls of volcanic rock for Blanc's *mur vegetals* are modern-day follies that await new plantings.
OVERLEAF: Wild grasses near the English-style river promenade.

Private Paris

The real voyage of discovery is not in seeking new
landscapes but in having new eyes.
Marcel Proust

Surrealism Near Madeleine

Le Corbusier's famous terrace reprised

Any urban garden is intrinsically surreal, but for his extraordinary 8th arrondissement eighteenth-century garret, American architect Michael Herrman chose architect Le Corbusier's odd 1929 Champs-Élysées penthouse and rooftop terrace for eccentric bon vivant Charles de Beistegui as a model of "Modern minimalism balanced with the playful extravagance of Surrealism."

Corbusier's historic terrace is gone but photographs show how its high railings obscured all but the tallest landmarks from view while a periscope, installed in de Beistegui's penthouse, popped upwards to look at city views. In the terrace, a fireplace and an oval mirror above it, a stone replica of a wooden commode alongside garden chairs and a parrot on a bird perch atop a "carpet" of lawn were all archetypal symbols of domesticity used to blur the line between "inside" and "outside."

Herrman removed the walls between a dozen stacked maids' rooms to form his sixth- and seventh-floor duplex under the eaves, and then added steel framing for a clear glass ceiling above the living area to bring daylight to both levels from a light well between the L-shaped apartment and two neighbors' walls.

While Corbusier obscured views, Herrman emphasized them. He used clear 10-by-10-foot sheets of fixed and sliding glass partitions to link the interior to the light well, now reconfigured as a minuscule courtyard filled with modern room furnishings and de Beistegui-esque motifs such as a birdcage, a gilt-framed mirror and garniture atop a marble fireplace.

Herrman's open-to-the-sky tableau in its 20-foot-high "vitrine" has another exciting difference—a vertical garden inspired by botanist Patrick Blanc's *mur vegetal* for the Musée du Quai Branly, where Herrman had assisted the museum's architect, Jean Nouvel. Its vines and herbaceous foliage hanging on the neighbor's windowless wall make it easy to believe that the fake patch of grass in the courtyard, sprouting in between woven vinyl replicas of the apartment's original hexagonal terra-cotta tiles, is real.

The young designer also devised a hi-tech periscope—a rooftop digital camera—that live-streams views of the Eiffel Tower and nearby Madeleine Church, as well as the occasional bird flying overhead, into a monitor camouflaged as a framed mirror on the dining room's ancient stone wall.

"I wanted to play," Herrman said, "with the idea of inside and outside, upstairs and downstairs and past and present as surreal reflections of each other."

PREVIOUS OVERLEAF: A species of green, brown and blackish spotted *Begonia blancii* named after its discoverer, botanist Patrick Blanc.
ABOVE: A bronze chandelier with solar-powered, waterproof LED bulbs encased in resin lights the vertical garden at night.
FACING: Naoto Fukasawa's Déjà-vu dining chairs and a mirror-top table literally and figuratively reflect the garden's theme.
OVERLEAF AND SECOND OVERLEAF: The courtyard seen from both floors. The custom woven vinyl and "grass" tiles are by Bolon and the tree-stump stools on the glass floor inside are by Herrman.

Louis Benech in Faubourg Saint-Germain

Bringing lights to a dark garden

The plan of this relatively small rectangular garden for a family with children living on the ground floor of a nineteenth-century Neoclassical building in Paris's aristocratic 7th arrondissement, near the Musée Rodin, is formal, to suit the house, but uncomplicated.

"These days there are fewer people to maintain a classic garden with perfect lawns and elaborate *parterres*. My approach is to make beautiful gardens that are simpler to take care of," its designer, Louis Benech, said.

Benech, a gardener and plants man at heart, who has famously tackled Le Nôtre's *jardins à la française* at the Tuileries and the first new *bosquet* at Versailles in centuries, is familiar with grand gardens with no armies of gardeners. Sans maintenance, nature claims them quickly, therefore formal gardens have to be planned well so if care lags "they look wilder but not rotten," he said.

This garden, with its existing lawn, is casual, yet sophisticated strategies were needed to make it so.

Benech "painted" sunny patches in the dark, tree-canopied north corner of the garden—an outdoor room—with plants, in his palette since the 1970s when he started gardening in England. "Yellow leaves give life to shaded areas," Benech said. The lighter silhouettes of *Catalpa bignonioides* 'Aurea', with heart-shaped leaves, lacier *Robina pseudoacacia* 'Frisia', with ovoid leaves, and *Weigela* 'Briant Rubidor' shrubs against dark, fast-growing *Iris* 'Tuxedo' evergreens planted in back, for privacy from the street just behind the garden wall, look sunny even on gloomy days.

The lawn, edged with stone, has expressionistic, free-form groupings of feathery and full-bodied shrubs on three sides, and irises and other flowers soften the formality of tall clipped hedges—a Benech signature—that screen lawn furniture from view. Clipped globes of *Quercus ilex,* like giant boule balls, land in corners.

The end of the garden "will get increasingly denser and cocoon-like in time," Benech said. The color of low blue-gray shrubs there "affect your sense of scale too," and make the grove feel deeper and more elegant.

"Le Nôtre's goal was to make large distances seem smaller," Benech said. "Mine is to extend the perspective."

FACING: The mottled bark of a plane tree is complemented by lacy *Robina pseudoacacia* 'Frisia' behind it.

TOP: Against a sidewall, a "bouquet" of clipped and unclipped shrubs.

RIGHT: Yew hedges on each side of the alcove double as screens.

OVERLEAF: The symmetrical room has lively asymmetrical plantings.

An Artful Hideout

A metal canopy offers shelter from the glare of fame

Landscape designer Louis Benech and Pierre Bergé, the celebrated arts patron and the erstwhile partner of the late fashion designer Yves Saint Laurent, met serendipitously at La Vallée Blonde, a nursery in Normandy where a young Benech worked as a horticulturist.

Bergé was equally passionate about plants, clearly evidenced by La Datcha, a Russian-style folly with two and a half rolling acres at his Chateau Gabriel in Benerville-sur-Mer, Normandy, and by his restored Majorelle Garden in Marrakech, and so, the two stayed in touch. A few years later, when Bergé's garden behind his *hôtel particulier* apartment on Rue Bonaparte in Paris needed revamping, Benech and Pascal Cribier, who had just begun their large commission to renovate Le Nôtre's Tuileries Garden nearby, happily took on the challenge in 1992.

LEFT: A striped, faux-canvas, metal canopy above the gravel terrace shelters potted bulbs and also makes it possible to use the terrace for dining outdoors. Beyond it, what looks like lawn is actually the top of a wide, three-foot-high rectangular hedge.
BELOW: A grouping of white painted benches and octagonal glass gazebos at each end of the canopy form rooms outdoors.
OVERLEAF: Bergé's prized orchids and tillandsias in the greenhouse.

Bergé's east-facing garden in Saint-Germain-des-Prés near the Seine was an odd triangular shape, cut from a rectangular courtyard that had been divided diagonally, and it had "only a few boxwood balls, a huge decaying poplar, shrubs and plants of no interest," Benech said.

All that was removed, and with the ground-floor neighbor's permission, matching linden trees planted on each side of the diagonal fence combined the two gardens visually. For greater diversity the designers added a Japanese varnish and a Judas tree, and thinned acacias, dogwoods and magnolias that let light through.

Within its oddball boundaries, the garden was reconfigured into two wide terraces parallel to the house, and an informal section for the plants Bergé avidly collects.

A new gravel-covered dining terrace steps down into a slightly lower terrace paved with stone slabs interspersed with foxgloves, astilbes, thalictrums, anemones and white blooming veronicastrums. On its far side, three steps lead up to the last level that brings showy camellias, mahonias and tree peonies into view. Pots containing colorful annuals, perennials and Peruvian or South African bulbs such as scilla and schizostylis, and, here and there, pruned balls of privet add life to the garden. The south end has potted conical topiaries and painted white wood benches to sit in the morning sun.

For winter protection, Bergé added a striped, faux-canvas, metal canopy above the gravel terrace and octagonal glass gazebos at each end. The canopy also protects delicate potted specimens, bamboos and ferns, while a greenhouse in back is home to Bergé's coveted orchids and tillandsias.

However, the introduction of four large rectangular slabs of hedging, all clipped to the same height, is the design's tour de force. These three-foot-high planes of greenery look like lawns from certain angles and visually unify all three sections into one large garden.

The spaces between the hedges form paths along which are fountains and—as nods to Bergé's passion for plants as well as art—a classical marble or two, tole works by Carmen Almon, a painter from the south of France who crafts sheet metal into fascinating botanically correct facsimiles of flowers, and the occasional red *Helleborus orientalis* 'Pierre Bergé' is a hat tip cultivated by none other than Normandy's renowned nurserywoman Martine Lemonnier.

TOP: A potted willow-leaved pear in the center of the stone-paved terrace creates a silvery focal point from every angle of the garden.
LEFT: Tole flowers in the garden are by botanical artist Carmen Almon.
FACING: East of the gravel court are the middle terrace and, in the distance, the garden's last tier. The large hedges blur their boundaries.

Hôtel George V Courtyard

Floriferous wonders by Jeff Leatham

The chic, palatial Four Seasons Hôtel George V near the Arc de Triomphe in the 8th arrondissement was the brainchild of its first owner, American hotelier Joel Hillman, who built it during the late 1920s heyday of transatlantic ocean liners and gave it its raison d'etre. Codesigned by French Beaux Arts architect Georges Wybo, the hotel's enormous marbled foyer, spacious anteroom and, beyond it, an immense interior courtyard were deliberately large to receive many guests and their large cabin trunks at once.

Today, the foyer as well as the generous 7,000-square-foot courtyard are the playground of the hotel's artistic director, florist Jeff Leatham, another American in Paris whose theatrical and even surreal flower arrangements are essentially contemporary gardens for a day or week, composed indoors and outdoors of masses of irises, hydrangeas, roses, calla lilies and orchids, or whatever seasonal flower the artist chooses for floor or table displays. To create the feeling of a garden in bloom and "add fullness to an arrangement," Leatham said, his flowers are often suspended or displayed at an angle. Sometimes, calla lilies bunched together and tilted dramatically in clear standing vases that showcase long green stems—a Leatham signature—are substituted for blossoms inverted into vases to magnify them under water. People are drawn inward by these inventive displays to Le Cinq and Le Galerie restaurants that open onto the courtyard, and this phenomenon alone may have prompted imitators to view flower displays as more than mere decoration.

The scale of Leatham's monochromatic, sculptural, garden-like "floral experiences" is always large to counter the lofty chandelier-lit volumes of the George V's classic interior as well as the open-to-the-sky courtyard that has some of the best rooms looking down onto it.

One April, purple orchids grouped together in several black ball vases were paired with an ethereal canopy of more orchids—roots and all—suspended between the hotel walls and a metal-and-frosted-glass cascade fountain that flowed into a shallow pool lined with reflective silver panels in the middle of the courtyard. The Alhambra-esque display entertained diners sitting around it under classic black umbrellas or within curtained cabanas in the marble-covered space, where raised beds containing river rock and boxwood topiaries at each corner provided islands of privacy in Leatham's ever-changing "garden."

FACING: The George V's interior courtyard with a canopy of purple orchids is a typical over-the-top display by Jeff Leatham.
ABOVE: In the foyer, an arrangement of lilies, hydrangeas and votive candles in clear vases forms a floral "chandelier."
OVERLEAF: Close-ups of the suspended orchids, fountain and reflecting pool lined with silvered panels in the courtyard.

Kenzo Takada's Perfect Retreat

A Japanese-style garden in the Bastille lives on

The quiet garden that fashion designer Kenzo Takada and his landscape architect Iwaki installed nearly 25 years ago still looks as good as on the day it was completed. A pool of water laps around islands of greenery, and tall bamboo on the outer edges of the 1,000-square-foot garden filters afternoon light and casts dappled shadows. It also shields neighbors from view, enhancing the illusion that the garden is not in the busy center of Paris but on some island in Japan.

Coincidentally, Takada's 14,000-square-foot wood-and-glass home designed by Kenji Kawabata and Xavier de Castella—replete with an authentic Japanese tearoom by Mizusawa Komuten and a wood sitting porch cantilevered over the garden's koi-filled pond—rose on one of the largest lots near the Bastille where a warehouse of gardening equipment once stood. Takada bought the warehouse and its contents, supplemented them with new materials from Japan and imported Japanese craftspeople to reshape this corner of Paris into a place where he could sit far from the flash of fashion. Even a water basin scooped out of a cylindrical stone column near the sitting porch is for ancient tea ceremonies in the garden.

A wall of tall steel-and-glass doors in the living room opens to French oak wood decks that jut out toward the naturalistic "shores" of moss, lichens, junipers and river rock. Built-in banquettes with long white cushions double as a railing wall for a heated indoor swimming pool, but also provide a view across the living room at the patio and the garden.

However, unlike conventional French gardens designed for classic *hôtels particuliers* as big as this home, this garden has no symmetrical arrangements or long perspective views. Instead it relies on juxtapositions of forms and textures and the interplay of light and sound. The garden is a shimmering tapestry of light and dark greens, seasonal pink cherry blossoms and plum red Japanese maples. Perfectly placed boulders are interspersed with grasses, and water falls between them into pools flecked with darting red koi.

Ironically, the house now belongs to Pascal Breton, a well-known writer, television film producer and founder of Marathon Images, and it is often flooded with friends invited to lavish costume parties. Only the garden, recently restored with the help of Zen garden designer Erik Borja, remains as a zone of total repose.

FACING: The entry court to Kenzo Takada's former home in the Bastille, with wood and bronze guardians near the door.
ABOVE: A wood patio from the living room juts out into a koi pond and garden filled with moss, bamboo, junipers and rock.
OVERLEAF, LEFT: A view of the Japanese tearoom and meditation deck.
OVERLEAF, RIGHT: Detail of waterfalls that enliven the garden.
SECOND OVERLEAF, LEFT: The indoor swimming pool has garden views.
SECOND OVERLEAF, RIGHT: A moss-covered island in the koi pond.

Follies at Villa André Bloc

Combining art, architecture and nature

Art, ubiquitous in the French garden, is also present in this roughly one-acre garden in Meudon, an idyllic suburb southwest of Paris. In 1952, French architect André Bloc, who admired Le Corbusier and was closely aligned to the visionary spatial ideas of architect Claude Parent, built himself a boomerang-shaped stone-and-concrete home and studio. In the foyer between the two wings of Villa André Bloc, a curved wall of glass panels framed in steel was aimed toward an existing picturesque rear garden that went up a wooded hill overlooking the Seine Valley.

LEFT: André Bloc's 1959 cast-brass sculpture in a picturesque setting.
BELOW: From the foyer, a view of the pool and up-sloping garden.
A mosaic tiled wading pool is outside the curved steel-and-glass wall.
OVERLEAF: Bloc's 1964 white *Sculpture Habitacle II* with a resin door.

An amoeba-shaped pool in the middle of the up-sloping lawn was the only significant addition to the garden until the mid-1960s, when Bloc, who was also a sculptor and the founder of influential art and architecture journals, decided to make bigger changes. He wished to give shape to his evolving notions of space that went from 1920s-style geometric neo-plasticism to the sort of free-form expressionism that artist Jean Arp, who also lived in Meudon, liked. Like Arp, who said, "One has to create like nature," Bloc was increasingly drawn to enigmatic, organic shapes.

"Formerly, cities were marked with greatly pleasing and vast sculptural elements. In the improvisation of temporary cities, the value of such elements has been forgotten," Bloc once wrote. He yearned for the poetry of prewar cities not blighted by merely expedient, efficient modernity, and so, not surprisingly, he brought the sculptural dome and tower of ancient cities like his native Algiers into his own garden.

Bloc's sculptural musings in plaster led to two handmade follies of brick dubbed *Sculptures Habitacles* that are a cross between sculpture and architecture that is usable but not habitable.

In 1964, Bloc completed a white painted brick "dome" called *Sculpture Habitacle II* on the lawn behind his villa. This thick-walled, roughly 1,000-square-foot cubistic folly with folds, creases and odd window perforations looks like a grouping of primitive African masks derived from skull shapes. Its cathedral-like vaulted interior, where its current owner, gallerist Natalie Seroussi, sometimes organizes art installations and performances, is suffused with a dim light filtered through a translucent amber resin door and iridescent mica "window" coverings.

The second folly, *Sculpture Habitacle III, La Tour,* a Dubuffet-esque red brick tower completed in 1966—the same year as Bloc's accidental death in New Delhi, India—is a vertical labyrinth of dead ends, ramps and stairs that eventually get to the tower's summit. Hidden amid trees on the hill, this totemic 80-foot-high work is perhaps an ironic metaphor for life and an instrument, with its several balconies and a top deck, to see farther than the surrounding woods and the last vestiges of vast historic gardens André le Nôtre designed for nearby Chateau de Meudon, which was destroyed in a fire.

Bloc's mysterious follies mark the successful evolution of his sculpture from geometric abstract shapes to free-form volumes that, if they evoke natural caverns and primitive caves, were exactly what Bloc intended. "With my work," he wrote, "I seek to unite man with his environment in warmer, more personal ways."

ABOVE: Espaliered fruit trees are scattered within the woods where *Sculpture Habitacle III, La Tour* was completed in 1966. The Dubuffet-esque tower is an 80-foot-high labyrinth with an internal staircase that, on the way to the top, has several dead-end ramps and protruding balcony landings. The highest deck has panoramic views of the Seine Valley.
FACING: An east view of the woods. Sol LeWitt's white *Incomplete Cube* in the foreground complements Bloc's *Sculpture Habitacle II,* which, like Picasso's cubist works, was inspired by African masks.

Jean-Michel Othoniel's *Herbier*

Coded messages in a Mariais garden

"My passion for flowers began during my adolescence," French sculptor Jean-Michel Othoniel explained, grateful to an erudite uncle in rural Saint-Étienne, where he grew up, for making him think of gardens as places filled with stories.

That's why a U-shaped, 1,600-square-foot roof garden, above the two top floors of a nineteenth-century building with a central courtyard in the Marais where he and Belgian sculptor Johan Creten live and work, is also a botanical trove of information.

"The first religious symbols, even before they were painted, came directly from nature, and of those, flowers were the first," Othoniel said. In *L'Herbier Merveilleux: Notes sur le sens caché des fleurs dans la peinture* (The Wonderful Herbarium: Notes on the hidden meaning of flowers in paintings), a little volume by Othoniel in which he describes visits to Italian gardens where he

LEFT: Othoniel and Creten's roof deck garden has roses for cutting.
BELOW: A window box garden wraps around their home below the busy atelier, which is directly under the roof garden.
OVERLEAF: Red painted Tectona deck chairs, designed for transatlantic steamers, were handpicked to match the garden's summer colors.

first gleaned the sacred meanings of flowers and trees, he also describes *coquelicots,* or red poppies, that he grows. In church gardens they were symbols of Christ's martyrdom, and in historic battlefields that became parks they were proud emblems of patriotism.

For his garden, Othoniel tracks down flowers vested with symbols, such as blue *Veronica filiformis,* which is a good medicinal ground cover with two dark pistils that represent the eyes of Christ imprinted on Sainte Véronique's scarf, the five-petalled pale eglantine (*Rosa canina*), which represents Christ's patience, and fine, pendulous *Fuchsia magellanica* blossoms, that allude to the Virgin Mary's earrings.

Classical myths that the Renaissance revived are embedded in plants like the laurel, which represents the bitter metamorphosis of Apollo's Daphne. Red *Anemone*

ABOVE AND RIGHT: Flea market furniture is combined with varied clay and white fiberglass pots. Purple *Iris germanica* represents the daughter of Electra and celestial messenger of the gods.

coronaria represents Aphrodite's grief over Adonis's spilled blood, while Othoniel's thriving *Ficus carica*, the fig tree sacred to Chronos, Hermes and Dionysus, is the classical symbol of peace and immortality.

Recently, Othoniel and Creten exhibited their nature-inspired works alongside Delacroix's floral paintings that are rife with symbols of dissidence and political unrest at the Musée Delacroix, and at Versailles, Othoniel unveiled the first new and permanent additions to the royal park in centuries. His three interpretive fountains are in the Water Theater Grove, Le Nôtre's woodland *bosquet* that was completely reimagined in 2014 by landscape designer Louis Benech. Although Othoniel's inspiration for the fountains came from a book where Louis XIV's waltz moves are shown as calligraphic, arabesque patterns, it is believed that those patterns were also replicated in *parterres de broderie* at Versailles.

Floral sources aren't immediately obvious in Othoniel's conceptual sculptures that sometimes resemble gravity-defying giant necklaces composed of metal underpinnings and blown-glass beads the size of bowling balls. However, like gardens, his works, such as the Palais Royal subway entrance canopy, are preoccupied with transience and death, and are simultaneously decorative, glittering, beautiful and ultimately as delicate as flowers.

Had Othoniel's dream of a garden "in the ground" been realized he would have had big trees too. "My grandmother had a potager where I watered apple, cherry and apricot trees like the ones we have," he added, pointing to the dwarfed medley in his collection. Nonetheless, there are plans to extend the garden into an unused section of the roof where more trees in pots, and flea market finds such as Victorian cast iron furniture, will complement the predominantly pink oasis.

"I don't think there is a perfect color but I think pink is easier to combine with the flowers I grow for cutting," Othoniel said. Among his favorites are *Rosa sp.* roses, beloved of Sainte Thérèse de Lisieux, and *Paenoia officinalis* peonies, considered—take your pick—the rose of the Pentecost or a cure for madness. Red painted wood Tectona deck chairs, designed for transatlantic steamers, were chosen to match colors in the late summer and fall when the pink *Hydrangea paniculata* is full, the apples turn red and—most importantly—the busy sculptors have time to rest.

FACING: A flea market Medusa and owl amid pots and plants.
TOP: A birdbath stands next to roses seen against Marais rooftops.
RIGHT: Growing under an apple tree, a wild *Fragaria vesca,* which often appears in nativity scenes for its strawberries and white flowers that represent Christ's blood and humility.

Up on the Roof

Couturier Martin Grant's mini Marais estate

Fashion designer Martin Grant, whose grandmother taught him the joys of gardening in his native Australia, delights in his country-style garden outside a top-floor loft in Paris's space-starved pre-Haussmann Marais area.

The 9-by-12-foot terrace just off the living space is jammed with hardy boxwood topiaries, stone statuary, creeping ivy and an arched grapevine at the far end, as well as camellias, roses and bulbs in pots. Squares of ipe wood decking provide a maintenance-free surface over roofing, and the apartment's C-shaped configuration allows him the added benefit of a switchback view of an evergreen garden from his bedroom under the eaves.

Neighboring roof surfaces are also annexed since the sun shines on those spots at different times of year and frequent plant rotation results in a better tomato harvest.

"Do I privilege plants or people?" Grant wondered at the start. So zinc flower boxes doubling as railings contain tall hedges of rosemary and lavender on two sides of the terrace that is just large enough for a steel cafe table for two or five, if the party expands. An extra banquette with cloth-covered cushions is against a wall.

"Now I can spend an entire weekend there," he said.

LEFT AND BELOW: A verdant garden view from Grant's garret room.
OVERLEAF: The clipped, contained garden has enough space to sit in.

Contemporary Folly

An oasis of privacy at the Mandarin Oriental

The Mandarin Oriental Hotel in Paris's bustling fashion district opens onto a central courtyard at the end of a long, covered entryway and lobby off Rue Saint-Honoré. Architects Wilmotte & Associés and landscape designers François Neveux and Bernard Rouyer have provided a de rigueur green wall of drooping succulents in planter boxes that seem to cascade down the revamped Art Deco landmark, and a slender reflecting pool dissects the surprisingly intimate garden of ferns and evergreen shrubs that include Asian camellias. However, the standout destination in the garden is a giant, painted white steel birdcage containing a chandelier of stylized hot pink blossoms and upholstered fiberglass banquettes atop a stepped wood dais. This whimsical, allusive "Table du Jardin," created by Patrick Jouin and Sanjit Manku of the firm Jouin Manku, who also designed adjacent restaurants, is a contemporary folly echoing precedents at Désert de Retz and at Charles de Beistegui's eccentric 1930s Chateau de Groussay.

"This is a twenty-first-century palace," Manku said. "And luxury here," Jouin added, "'nests' in such details."

LEFT AND BELOW: Birdcage folly at the Mandarin Oriental Hotel, Paris.

Patrick Blanc's Jungle Inside

An ecosytem for a vertical garden

There is no more flamboyant scientist-botanist than green-haired Patrick Blanc, who perfected the *mur vegetal*, or vertical garden, as a teenager and later developed it to nurture plant specimens collected on cliffsides and steep slopes within the tropics. On one expedition to the Philippines he also discovered a new species of green, brown and blackish spotted flowers, named *Begonia blancii* after him.

"I started vertical gardens in my bedroom when I was 15 while trying to remove excess nitrogen and nutrients from my aquarium and giving it to plants instead," Blanc said.

His hydroponic solution for growing ferns, mosses, flowers, climbers and shrubs—never vines, "because they grow too much and cover everything"—on layers of

BELOW AND RIGHT: Temperate and tropical plants grow on three walls of botanist Patrick Blanc and singer Pascal Heni's entry court-yard, and in indoor and outdoor showers on the floor above it.
OVERLEAF: Another view of the entry courtyard and a close-up, indoors, of *Ficus villosa* growing flat against mosses in the shadows.
SECOND OVERLEAF, LEFT: Hanging roots soaking in a beaker.
SECOND OVERLEAF, RIGHT: Bookshelves reflected in the aquarium, which is Blanc's "living library" filled with plants, fish and frogs.

water-absorbent polyamide felt attached to PVC shields affixed to a metal armature that allows air to flow between it and the walls relies on nutrient-rich water drip-fed through tubes from the top and recirculated from a catch basin below. This kind of ecosystem has been replicated for outdoor vertical gardens worldwide in cities such as San Francisco, where Blanc's largest American *mur vegetal* is at Drew School. Paris has many more, in-

ABOVE: Blanc's 25-foot-high living room *mur vegetal* touches the peak. Light-seeking shrubs like berberis and cotoneaster are up high, while herbaceous heuchera and campanula grow lower.
LEFT: Water-seeking roots of succulents and other plants appear exposed on the surface of the *mur vegetal* outdoors.
FACING: Blanc's desk sits on top of the large aquarium that provides nutrient-rich water for the wall. Some plants emerge from a slot in the glass. Behind the desk is a drooping-fingered *Iris japonica*.

cluding one at the Musée du Quai Branly and another with 7,600 plants, arranged in Blanc's signature wavy bands, at L'Oasis d'Aboukir in the 2nd arrondissement.

However, Blanc's first major indoor vertical garden, built more than 30 years ago, is his own. It has sections containing cherished personal finds such as a *Ficus villosa* from Malaysia and has been moved thrice since 1982. At its latest location in the lofty living room of the home he shares with singer Pascal Heni in the south of Paris near Porte de Choisy, tiny tropical insectivore pet birds flit in and out of nearly 300 plants fed from a wall-to-wall, 5,300-gallon, two-foot-high aquarium. Its glass top is tough enough to hold Blanc's desk at one end, and on the opposite side are shelves full of botany journals where wandering garden lizards lurk.

"My books are quite safe," Blanc joked, "because lizards don't read."

The wall of books is also literally and figuratively reflected in the warm water "reservoir" that is home to a "living library" of 1,000 fish and plants.

Blanc has improvised similar watering systems for about 600 large-leaved specimens growing on three walls of his entry courtyard, and in indoor and outdoor showers and passageways on the second floor. Some plant roots trail straight down from upstairs to water-filled beakers beside the aquarium.

This inventive Parisian has succeeded in replicating hardy "gardens" on cliff walls and slopes that are only fed by sunshine, wind energy, ambient moisture, trickling dew and rain, and his unique soilless versions require only a little care. "As long as there is humidity, vertical gardens can grow anywhere. In hot areas they even absorb sunlight and keep buildings cool," Blanc said. "All they really need is water."

Camille Muller's Call of the Wild

A rooftop potager and its counterpart

"Listen to Nature," was landscape architect Camille Muller's mantra, long before he met landscape theorist Gilles Clément, his most influential mentor. A child of Alsace, where the mountains suffer harsh winters, Muller instinctively translated what he knew from the first vegetable patch in his parents' garden to moss gardens and rugged landscapes for Paris terraces that had to contend with strong sun, wind or too much shade.

His gardens were micro-ecosystems tuned to local conditions, vegetation and soil, and around 1978, when only classically beautiful gardens were considered good, his wildly naturalistic compositions with keen organic underpinnings, now de rigueur in today's best gardens, grew well, as did his reputation.

Sculptor César, painter Peter Klasen, clothing designer Marithé + François Girbaud and the Rothschild family found his work and his ideas beautiful, and more clients followed, with large-scale projects in Normandy, Burgundy and elsewhere.

In Paris it really began at his little-seen 1,200-square-foot loft atelier in the 11th arrondissement near the Bastille. It needed serious additions, such as real flooring and bathrooms, and Muller plugged away at it, and even installed a courtyard garden and potted palms in its skylit living area where his desk is. With Clément's encouragement, a garden on its sloped roof took shape.

This remarkable, organic, abundant, ecological project from the mid-'80s, engulfing its urban "canyon" setting between neighboring buildings, was the first of many more refined, structured versions, including, more than a decade later, the courtyard at Hôtel Costes on Paris's fashionable Rue Saint-Honoré.

Accessed by a spiral staircase from inside the loft and an odd ladder of zinc that goes up to its highest tier, Muller's utopian garden has small fruit trees, flowering vines, strawberries and other edible wonders in pots and bins. Tall *Semiarundinaria fastuosa* bamboo has also grown above the roofline from Muller's open-to-the-sky courtyard garden below, conjoining the two gardens.

His ingenious response to technical challenges—he had to worry about overloading the roof and sealing it properly, and bringing warm water to the plants—became a kind of solar-powered plant-growing system based on natural habitats, and birds and bees took to it readily. They became cogardeners, seeding the roof garden with snapdragons, cotoneasters and geraniums that did not have to be lugged upstairs. For them,

FACING: Camille Muller's tiered rooftop garden and potager has a zinc stair and ramp near a clothesline. *Semiarundinaria fastuosa* bamboo shoots up from an open-to-the-sky courtyard garden.
ABOVE: Ivy, *Akebia quinata* and *Parthenocissus quinquefolia* vines colonize a neighbor's wall in this old Parisian neighborhood.
OVERLEAF: A welcoming birdhouse amid climbing roses and ivies.

Muller built little birdhouses with his newfound carpentry and plumbing skills atop copper pipe totems, amid ivies and climbing roses.

When the time came about 15 years ago to expand the rooftop potager, and to really get his "hands into the ground," Muller settled on the rear section of a communal hillside lot next to Père Lachaise cemetery in the 20th arrondissement. It was the last corner of a royal hunting park saved by a group of environmentalists.

He enriched his potager organically, just as his grandparents and parents had done in the Colmar region. Replete with an artful Kandinsky-esque tool shed, and a blue cabin renovated by zinc artisan Francis Arsène that is a welcome shelter during bad weather, the potager relies on an eco-cycle of compost made from kitchen scraps that yields sumptuous seasonal produce. Muller, when he isn't pampering the tomatoes, raspberries, arugula, watercress and a fig tree among other delights, creates ornaments, windmills and abstract sculpture from castaway wood and other finds to entertain friends who visit his potager, which is also his playground. They are scattered among flowering bushes, roses trained on bamboo scaffolding and flowering *Phygelius capensis* that is cushioned by voluptuous clipped balls of boxwood that bring some order and architecture to what might seem like chaos to the uninitiated.

LEFT AND BELOW: An artful painted tool shed, wood stumps and wrought iron finds add sculptural notes to a jumble of flowers and tomato vines creeping up bamboo scaffolding in the potager.
OVERLEAF, LEFT: In the foreground, red *Phygelius capensis* in bloom.
OVERLEAF, RIGHT: Architectural boxwood balls flank a narrow path to Muller's blue cabin remodeled by Francis Arsène.

Chimneys and Sweeping Views

Rich ground for a Mediterranean garrigue

On the western edge of Paris, a duplex in a nondescript building overlooking the Auteuil Hippodrome in the 16th arrondissement only had a small back deck, but its 1,400-square-foot roof terrace with a stunning view of the horse track on one side and the Eiffel Tower on the other was enviable. However, the owners rarely got to enjoy it because the tenth-floor terrace's windswept expanse of standard orange terra-cotta tiles was either too sunny in the summer or too windy in the winter.

Luckily, two black, glazed-brick chimney towers in opposing corners of the terrace provided some shelter, and landscape designer Camille Muller, who was hired to design a garden up there, absolutely loved them.

"I definitely did not want to camouflage them," Muller said. "They were beautiful graphic forms."

Muller's garden design philosophy, "to leave what exists intact and develop that," could not have been better tested, and he could not have been more ready to use it. "After working with many architects and artists during the last decade, I was interested in contemporary art and architecture too," he said.

A protégé of Gilles Clément, the well-known botanist and landscape theorist who invented naturalistic "gardens in movement," Muller leaned toward eco-friendly gardens too, but he was comfortable with more structured, architectural ones.

With such a hybridized design for the Auteuil home in mind, Muller reused the circular steel staircase connecting its back deck to the roof terrace. Francis Arsène, Muller's frequent collaborator and the owner of Arzinc, a company specializing in galvanized garden accouterments, gave the zinc staircase a sheathing that makes it look like staircases in some Le Corbusier buildings. The impressive chimneys became sculptural focal points at each end of an L-shaped wood deck that floated over a third of the rectangular terrace filled with French limestone pebbles. The top of the chimney tower on the southwest side was fitted with a stainless steel trellis to train wisteria into a leafy canopy for shade.

When it came to choosing plants, "I started as a beginner and experimented to see which plant adapted best," Muller said. A regular at Clément's La Vallée garden in Creuse, about 200 miles south of Paris, Muller understands "gardens in movement" well. They rely as much on a gardener's ability to understand the terrain as they do on their own tendency to "move" naturally in nomadic clumps each season. As if to prove his point

that the right plants won't fight the natural conditions of a site, bulbs and grasses in the roof garden at the Auteuil terrace wandered after a season or two into the gravel beyond their designated containers.

"All I did was stage the site with voids as well as filled spaces," Muller said.

Ten years later, Muller's hardy Mediterranean plants, picked because of the windy conditions on the terrace, all clearly like their habitat. Clipped *Phillyrea angustifolia* thrives in tall, tapered terra-cotta pots placed strategically close to or against the warm chimneys, or as wind barriers around wooden benches designed by architect Jean-Marc Millière. More wind- and drought-resistant species such as aromatic phillyreas and varieties of cistus flourish in pots or zinc planters by Arzinc. In the northwest corner of the garden, grasses and a twisted, wind-pollinated mountain pine in a rectangular raised bed—to evoke a buffeted island in the wind—complete Muller's successful Mediterranean garrigue.

LEFT: On the bench sides, tall tapered pots contain clipped *Phillyrea angustifolia* bushes. In the background, branches of a Bohemian olive (*Elaeagnus angustifolia*) and a view of the Auteuil Hippodrome.
BELOW: Behind the furniture designed by Jean-Marc Millière are *Elaeagnus ×ebbingei* shrubs and *Pennisetum alopecuroides* 'Herbstzauber' grass.

Hide-and-Seek Garden

A play structure forms a tiered wonderland

For landscape designer Hugues Peuvergne there could be no better compliment than the note of thanks that reads, the "children are in it *all* the time."

Peuvergne is convinced that the small rectangular garden he designed near Porte de la Muette in the 16th arrondissement succeeded because the family's three little children inundated him with questions about their play space when they spotted him on-site. "I took copious notes about what they wanted: a cabin, a fishing hole, places to run and, of course, jump!"

Peuvergne apprenticed with Camille Muller, who absorbed principles of the natural "garden in movement" from Gilles Clément, and here Peuvergne applied them in a lighthearted way—to make a very practical garden.

If modern homes are "machines for living," this designer's modern gardens are "machines for living well," and that includes dining, entertaining and, in this case, playing hide-and-seek.

The garden on three levels—born out of the biggest hurdle in the shape of a low retaining wall separating the 10-foot-wide paved patio, outside the ground-floor kitchen, from a nondescript sloped garden—is a dining court, with decks connected by short ladders, densely planted "jungle" pathways and square stepping "stones" on the slope for the children to romp on. Peuvergne made practical safety barriers invisible, and in the "woods," a "secret" cabin with portholes—a feature he often likes to use—is open, like a dollhouse, so that the children can be easily watched from inside the family home.

Except for a Mexican orange choisya tree that was saved, all the plantings are new, including a rockery full of herbs, a large-leaved *Fatsia japonica* that thrives in low light, hardy white flowering luzula rushes, *Erigeron karvinskianus,* ferns, salvias, showy clematis 'The President,' and subtle pink and white roses that mingle with light-colored *Phyllostachys aurea* and dark *Phyllostachys nigra* bamboo.

"Nothing is precious," Peuvergne said, and "so the children really do not have to be afraid to be themselves in such a garden."

FACING: The topmost tier has a tiny square Japanese-style koi pond.
TOP: A rockery opposite the open cabin contains kitchen herbs.
RIGHT: A bridge to the cabin goes past large-leaved *Fatsia japonica.*
OVERLEAF: The unique three-tiered garden made to fit the site is for an energetic "family in movement."

Rooftop Edens in the 16th

Hugues Peuvergne's outdoor rooms

Most Parisian terraces, especially in areas near the Place de Mexico, are transformed into some type of garden, but few are as lush, decorative or practical to relax in as this one designed by Hugues Peuvergne.

The 1,300-square-foot L-shaped terrace just off a sixth-floor apartment kitchen had potential but it was windy, too sunny on hot days, and its big, ugly railings and three massive blocks of chimneys broke up the space awkwardly. In that dense area full of Haussmannian buildings, several neighbors live at least a floor

BELOW: A cafe table in the entry court of this well-established 16th arrondissement L-shaped garden that has several discrete zones.
RIGHT: The garden has a potager with fruit trees at the far end.
OVERLEAF: Arbors leading to the dining terrace and the children's garden from the entry court.

higher, so visual privacy was important to the owners, who wanted a space where they could entertain friends or be with the family without all eyes upon them.

Peuvergne loves such challenges and the solution came to him quickly. "I decided to create a country-like setting in the city with several different destinations where the owners could walk under many plants and trees from one narrative to the next," he said.

Using the chimneys as natural dividers between sections, he created four distinct areas more or less in enfilade. The entry garden just off the kitchen leads to an outdoor dining area that flows into a children's garden with a cabin to hide in, and finally, around the bend awaits a potager with a square raised bed for vegetables in the center. Three pergolas attached to the chimneys and draped with flowering vines form arched entryways to the last three sections and, here and there, frosted pouch-shaped glass lanterns that hang in the arbors look decorative even during the day.

"Small gardens that are broken into smaller parts tend to feel much larger because you can vary the experiences in each area," Peuvergne said.

Within a few years, despite the wind, the well-acclimated garden became a jungle. A purple-leaved *Cotinus coggygria* 'Royal Purple' in a sea of green is like a central landmark. Hardy pink 'Claire Matin' and white rosa 'Iceberg' rose vines climb the pergolas, and in wood tubs and zinc drums, blue sage and *Viburnum opulus* grow around arbors and along the garden path. All these elements together form a cocooned environment that is comfortable year-round.

The children's cabin, a recurring feature in many of Peuvergne's gardens, is echoed again in the potager's toolshed. Harvests include lettuce, tomatoes, zucchini and aromatic herbs in abundance, as well as olives and apples, and when that happens, the owners love to throw a party.

"I like it when people tell me that I make good gardens but I like it best when they tell me that there was a party thanks to the garden," Peuvergne said, pleased that he hears this often.

The clearly successful terrace garden led to another commission from the same client for a slightly higher spot within the same building.

FACING: Flowering *Viburnum opulus* shrubs trained up arbors are seen from the children's garden facing the entry court.
TOP: A swing in the children's garden. Beyond it are a table and chairs in the dining alcove. The Eiffel Tower is visible in the distance.
RIGHT: The children's play cabin is in the foreground. Visible in the background is the coveted potager.

This 300-square-foot terrace had similar problems as the first. It was also ugly, sunny, windy and too exposed, but the owner wanted to see something completely different this time. He wanted a very private retreat for a rooftop bathtub with a view.

"Their architect could not fit a bathtub within the apartment so he just put it in an atrium on the roof," Peuvergne explained.

For privacy, and because this garden was about taking in the sky and city views in a quiet atmosphere, Peuvergne used low-budget corrugated zinc cladding for the railings to form a sleek, modern enclosure within which he created a Zen garden resembling a dry

riverbed with lightweight volcanic and pozzolan rocks.

Simple as it looks, the cement-tile terrace had to be prepared with a complex drainage system of two-inch-thick perforated polystyrene plates and covered with a filtering fabric before the low-density lava rocks—which had to be precisely weighed for load capacity—could be piled on. "The lava is extremely sharp so we had to have gloves to manipulate it or risk cuts during installation," Peuvergne said.

Besides winching these materials up seven floors from the side of the building, looking for just three trees for the arid garden was probably the most difficult task. "Less is more" may be the Modernist's dictum, but here less took a lot more time. Peuvergne visited a lot of nurseries looking for just the right trees until at last he found hardy *Chamaecyparis obtusa* 'Nana Gracilis', a slow-growing false cypress that had been cultivated to look as if it were sculpted by tempests. And it wasn't until a few years later that the spare desert landscape was given a counterpoint—and crowning touch—*Carex buchananii* grasses that dance in the wind.

FACING: A narrow stair leads up from the apartment to the tub with a view in its own private atrium. A small deck is just big enough for a single chaise longue.

BELOW: Red lava rock is arranged to resemble a dry riverbed. *Chamaecyparis obtusa* 'Nana Gracilis' evergreen pines of different heights and a row of grasses create a false perspective intended to make the small garden look longer.

A Crater with a View

A volcanic roof garden spills over the edges

In the evenings, with Sacré-Coeur glowing in the distance, this reddish fifth-floor roof-deck for a duplex near Place des États-Unis in the 16th arrondissement looks alien, like an undulating Martian landscape suddenly come to life.

"I like to think that it was planted by a few birds," its designer, landscape gardener Hugues Peuvergne said, although the dramatic garden was a figment of his imagination and made completely to his precise specifications.

What used to be a mundane, 500-square-foot cement tile–covered terrace is now a U-shaped garden contained in wide planters that wrap around a relatively small rectangular wood deck that appears sunken, but is on the same level as the adjacent kitchen floor. Its built-in bench with a red cushion and a light portable chaise

BELOW AND RIGHT: The multilayered modern garden by designer Hugues Peuvergne seems to bubble out of a volcanic crater.

are enough when the owner chooses to sit outside, although most of the time either the wind picks up or it gets too sunny for comfort.

That's largely why Peuvergne designed the garden not so much as a practical, usable space to be in—like the majority of his gardens are—but as a tableau to be enjoyed while dining inside the kitchen.

"Instead of a big space to be in, it was better in this case to look out at a big garden," the designer said.

That meant he could happily eliminate umbrellas and any kind of awning for shade that would have marred the view. It is instead very carefully framed by naturally twisted *Pinus sylvestris* and shaped *Pinus mugo* 'Mughus' pines at the northeast end of the garden. Thanks to other repairs being carried out on the building, the designer was even able to change clunky guard railings on all three sides to thin stretched steel cables that blend into the sky.

"It was also important to find the right plants that would pull the eye with each successive layer toward the famous landmark," Peuvergne said.

His limited plant palette includes lavender clipped low into cushions, creeping *Parthenocissus quinquefolia,* thyme, some bulbs, the occasional *Digitalis purpurea* and plenty of pink erodium 'Bishop's Form'. It all grows and crawls over mounds of red lava rock and pozzolan that is significantly less heavy than it looks.

A sliding glass wall now connects the kitchen literally and visually to the outside, which, despite its carefully tended look, never looks static from inside.

"We planned that," Peuvergne said, "and because we wanted the garden to be enjoyed from many rooms," the wild, volcanic landscape seems to bubble up and, quite literally, spills over the edges of the roof terrace onto ledges on the east side and a balcony one floor below, as if it were molten lava.

Regular clipping keeps the mainly evergreen garden that has spread over time seemingly unchanged throughout the year, as if earthly seasons don't exist, and yet, during the winter when there is a layer of fresh snow over it, the always-incredulous designer finds the garden "unexpectedly startling and even more beautiful."

LEFT: Windswept pines, clipped lavender bushes and low-to-the-ground creepers, planted to highlight a vista crowned by Sacré-Coeur, pop through layers of lightweight volcanic rock. Discreet up-lights are inset into each of the deck corners.
OVERLEAF, LEFT: The main garden that contains clipped lavender and a carpet of pink erodium "oozes" onto a balcony ledge, with a similar plant palette on the east side toward the Eiffel Tower.
OVERLEAF, RIGHT: A close-up of volcanic rock and *Allium christophii.*

Hugues Peuvergne at Play

A patient gardener vivifies his suburban yard

Landscape designer Hugues Peuvergne, a featured regular at France's best garden shows, is a protégé of Gilles Clément and Camille Muller, whose "gardens in movement" embrace the ways plants grow naturally. However, Peuvergne has strayed somewhat from these illustrious contemporaries and mentors.

"I also consider gardens to be in perpetual movement but I am not a conceptual designer," Peuvergne said. "I like to work with wild, spirited plants and shape them over time."

To best understand what he means by that is to enter the meticulously tended magical garden he has culti-vated for over two decades in Lagny-sur-Marne, about 15 miles east of Paris. It is a cross between the expertly clipped gardens the French are known for and a sylvan English landscape.

LEFT: A paved path from the gravel driveway leads to the garden behind Peuvergne's rustic one-story home behind a country villa.
BELOW: A flowering vine arches over the compound entrance where a driftwood totem marks the entrance to a bamboo *bosquet*.
OVERLEAF: The main villa is visible in the background. The garden, divided into three zones, has a dining area just outside Peuvergne's picture window on the right.

His 6,000-square-foot lot behind a suburban villa close to the river Marne was covered with thuja and rampant thorny berry bushes when he first saw it, but it appealed to him for a compact one-story house with whimsical outdoor rooms.

"Sometimes I like to tell a story with my gardens," Peuvergne explained. "This time I wanted a backdrop for children to let their imaginations run free," he said, recalling his parents' weekend house in the country where he used to disappear into nearby woods and think about gardens with tree houses.

With the power of his well-honed imagination he could see the garden fully formed through his home's large picture window before either one was even started.

LEFT: Clipped hedges cordon off the dining area above which a Canadian amelanchier offers ample summer shade. In the background is a bulbous clipped thuja "house," ostensibly for children.
BELOW: Ivy and bamboo grow freely on the garden's east side.

Peuvergne began with a dining terrace just off the future kitchen "because, while it is important to make a beautiful garden, it should also be beautiful to live in," he said. In time, his partner, Véronique Buard, and their children, who are both now nearly adults, got to experience exactly what he envisioned.

It was the overgrown thuja—leftover fencing material, and the bane of French gardeners who dislike it because it can be disease prone—which got the design started. Peuvergne kept it "because it was already mature and could be pruned easily," he said. He tamed the wild thuja into a *bosquet* next to the gravel driveway and into large balls in a lawn-covered garden on the far side of a short paved pathway between his house and a woodshed. More thuja, buxus and *Carpinus betulus* hornbeam hedges of various heights and shapes now subdivide the rectangular garden into three sequential sections that offer places in which to sit and dine, to run and also to hide.

On the west side of the garden is a bulbous tree house with two white oculi that is right out of a fairy tale. Children sit in there for hours. Made of a couple of thuja trees slowly trained and sculpted into a hollow form, it is probably Peuvergne's best-loved and most complex move in the garden.

"That took a lot of time and I really didn't want too much else to maintain," he admits. That's why some sections of the garden are left wilder than others, especially on the east side "where bamboo and other plants do what they want."

In the summer, when the whole family has more time in the garden, climbing 'Ghislaine de Féligonde' roses, clematis 'Piilu', *Geranium psilostemon*, salvias, valerians and other flowers add color, and a Canadian amelanchier with small purple fruit that birds love does double duty as a natural umbrella.

When the sun becomes too intense, Peuvergne rigs up an additional cloth canopy attached to an old telephone pole saved for just such a use. The garden has other castaways, such as birdcages hanging in trees, stone lanterns, driftwood totems and wrought iron fences, although none of it is considered art per se.

"I don't use sculpture in my gardens," Peuvergne said with emphasis. "The most important things in a garden should be plants."

FACING: Just off the dining deck, a carefully clipped thuja storybook "tree house" replete with oculi "eyes" and a potted topiary that stands in front of it that could be mistaken for a clown's nose.
TOP: Magical light spills onto the deck inside the living tree house.
RIGHT: A quaint country cabin that serves as a potting shed.

Montmartre Gallery Garden

MariCarmen Hernandez's arid, art-filled terrace

For Mexican architect, sculptor and painter MariCarmen Hernandez, who has lived in Paris for decades, city views and flowers in window boxes are garden enough. Her Montmartre rooftop could have been perfect for growing things, but considering that she travels half the year it would have been challenging. Instead, she decided to transform the terrace into an outdoor living room with pebble-and-cement floor tiles that resemble gravel-covered permaculture courts, and weatherproof, hand-shaped clay furniture. Add to these a collection of oddments including a recycled seat from a favorite car that died, an artful clay-and-glass coffee table she made and many of her large canvases that depict abstract versions of Paris skies, plants and gardens, and you get an uncommon gallery. Up there, she entertains friends or models that pose for the retablo-style portraits she has become known for. And if the conversation ever lags, "there is magnificent Sacré-Coeur Basilica to look at," she said.

LEFT AND BELOW: Stairs lined with Hernandez's portraits lead up to the terrace from the mesmerizing apartment.
OVERLEAF: Dinner guests get a prime view of Sacré-Coeur Basilica.
SECOND OVERLEAF: Hernandez's eclectic terrace furniture and art.

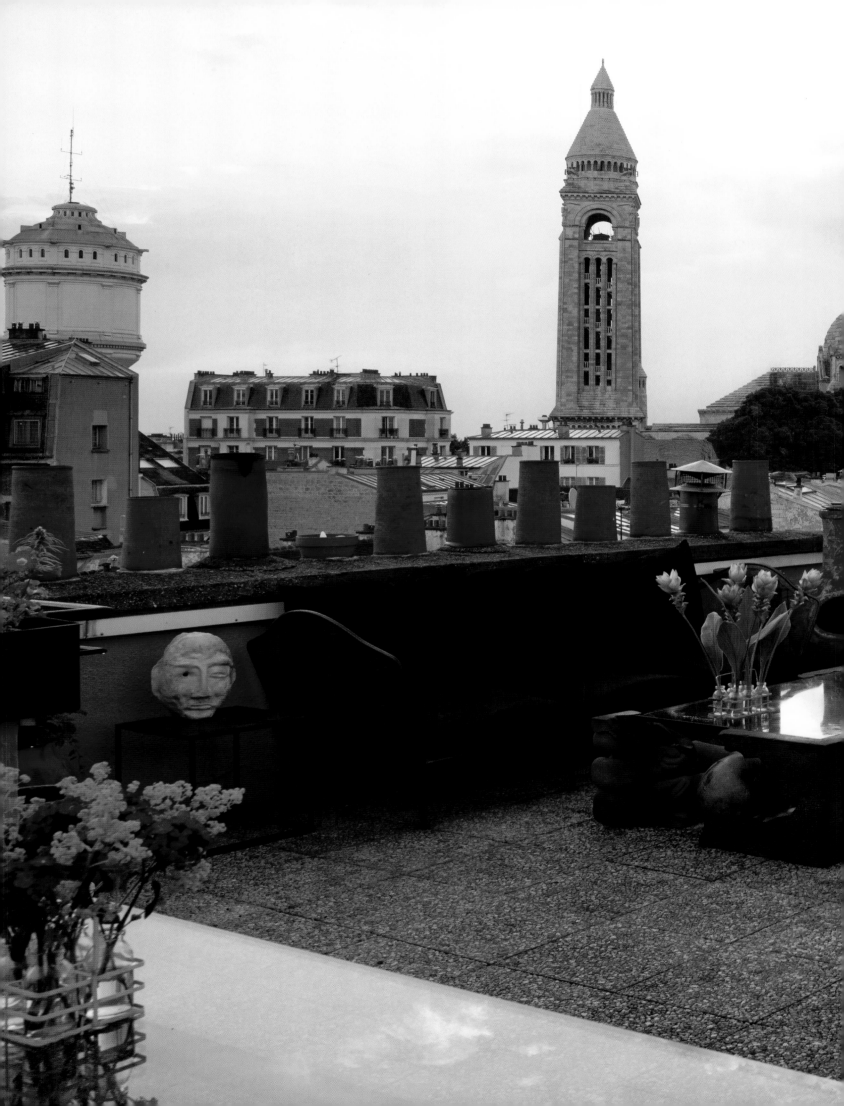

Where the Wild Things Are

Valentine Hansen de Ganay's urban jungle

Author Valentine Hansen de Ganay's 10th-floor mid-century penthouse in the 5th arrondissement, which she shares with her husband, artist Markus Hansen, and their three children, is not as ancient as her family's country estate at Courances, but it is nonetheless enviable.

High on a hill near Rue Mouffetard in the Left Bank, the apartment commands unparalleled views from a two-tiered terrace garden just off the salon. What's more, unlike ground-floor courtyard gardens in most Parisian multistory buildings that have to be shared, this aerial terrace can remain exclusively theirs.

Designed by the renowned landscape architect and designer Pascal Cribier, the roughly 3,000-square-foot garden rises above rooftops around it, and its panoramic view includes prominent landmarks such as

LEFT: Beyond a fig tree in the foreground, a central raised bed of corrugated aluminum sheeting with an olive tree in the middle allows for side aisles down the length of the terrace.
BELOW: The wire mesh pergola seen from the salon rooftop.
OVERLEAF: Plants and a mirrored chimney melt into the view.

the Montparnasse and Eiffel towers, and the Pantheon dome that crowns the tombs of Voltaire, Victor Hugo, and other luminaries. The nearby Jardin des Plantes, a botanical garden that was founded in 1626 as a royal medicinal garden during Louis XIII's reign, has over 10,000 species of plants, and some of these appear in the couple's terrace garden too.

To contain them, Cribier formed a central "bed" made of five-inch-thick, double-walled, corrugated aluminum sheeting over concrete pavers that are gently sloped toward a central drain. Sedums, euphorbias, carnations and fragrant lilies shaded by an olive tree at its center all coexist, happily attracting butterflies. Tall bins and cans along the railings contain climbing plants such as star jasmine, and espaliered fruit trees tethered to chimneys form green "walls" around the terrace. Woven rattan "fencing" attached to side railings acts as a wind barrier and, above the salon on a rooftop terrace that can be accessed by a ladder with grab rails, some hardy tamarisk trees in concrete planters ward off easterly winds.

A loose wire mesh stretched from the upper terrace to a central chimney on the lower terrace forms a lightweight pergola for shade-giving vines and creepers. Other chimney shafts that rise on the sides of the terrace are mirrored to reflect plants as well as views that, when seen through the mesh of foliage and windscreens, are like a Henri Rousseau painting come alive. Like Rousseau, the Fauvist who once said that exotic plants at the Jardin des Plantes made him think he was entering "into a dream," Cribier also enjoys "the visual disruption" of this parallel world. In his surreal slice of "nature," views get reversed, immovable landmarks change places like chess pieces and airplanes cross the open sky like migratory birds.

The garden is a whimsical experiential space where the owners can play with plant pairings as well as create a space for outdoor living that includes luxuriously decadent plein air showers, installed ostensibly for the children's use, against chimneys on the top deck.

Avid gardeners, the couple can always escape to their potager near vast water gardens at Courances that predate André Le Nôtre's most famous gardens. However, their collaboration with Cribier has formed another practical "getaway," de Ganay said. "Here, we can grow things for our table by just stepping outside."

LEFT, TOP: A close-up of common purslane for de Ganay's table.
LEFT: The brimming central bed sits atop concrete roof tiles.
FACING: Potted grasses cordon off an outdoor shower area on the salon rooftop that the children love to use on very hot days.

Outdoor Rooms

A surreal terrace for a whiff of the country

ABOVE: Looking from the small terrace through the penthouse.
FACING: The entry, past large black pots, into the smaller terrace.
FIRST OVERLEAF: The small terrace that is cooler most of the time has a mauve table, *Clematis armandii* in the pergola, *Acer griseum* and Japanese maple in large black pots also planted with white erigeron and roses, and weeds in the fake turf floor.
SECOND OVERLEAF: In the big terrace, more maples, common fig (*Ficus carica*), and purple-leaved *Cercis canadensis* grow in black pots, and reddish-pink valerian, oleander and herbs in a wood planting bed that has new treads cut in for easier access.

"Gardens are extra rooms for most people in Paris," Pierre-Alexandre Risser said. The animated garden designer, owner of Horticulture & Jardins in Saint-Prix and the cofounder of Jardins, Jardin, the progressive garden show in Paris that became heir to Aude de Thuin's L'Art du Jardin, has become justly famous for innovative terraces made for outdoor living.

When it comes to creating viable ecosystems for such gardens, Risser, the author of many how-to garden books, is a purist thanks to a childhood near the Lyon countryside and an education in agriculture and horticulture. "I have always been fascinated by plants, animals and ecology," Risser explained. His country garden, where he experiments with soils for favorite plants, is a laboratory to understand what can be grown even in adverse conditions.

So it comes as a shock to learn that Risser's secret for perfect green lawns for this terrace in Asnières-sur-Seine, just northwest of Paris, is artificial turf.

The clients wanted nothing but grass and "sometimes that is just not possible," the designer confessed.

The 800-square-foot terrace is divided into two unequal rectangular sections by a penthouse in the middle. Opposing doors on two sides of the living room visually connect the turfed spaces, of which the smaller 300-square-foot terrace faces northwest, and the larger, southeast.

A pergola of two-by-six-inch pine lengths for *Clematis armandii* vines, growing in square wood boxes, keeps the smaller terrace cooler in the summer. In black synthetic planters as big as the wood boxes, and in built-in boxes along concrete railing walls, Risser has also grown little white erigeron and Japanese maple. Small ovoid and long pointed leaves mingled with trailing vines create a lacy texture that is doubled by a mirror or two within the garden. A mauve cafe table and chairs add color in all seasons.

To continue the green, white and "pink" palette—which Risser finds most soothing in the shade of city gardens—the larger terrace has a wall-to-wall, waist-high, 6-by-30-foot wood container full of mauve valerian, white erigeron, *Nerium oleander* and herbs for the barbecue nearby.

The easy-care turf is extremely convincing, and the owners, a couple with a real garden in Burgundy, love it. Weeds, which add a touch of authenticity and the surreal, poke up through the "grass," and seem to like it too.

A Gardener's Retreat

Pierre-Alexandre Risser's country home

Even small urban gardens can be like "escapes to the country," Pierre-Alexandre Risser, the irrepressible, playful cofounder of Jardins, Jardin, the annual Paris garden show at the Tuileries, said.

Yet, because "there is nothing better than the real thing," the jaunty *paysagiste* for Kenzo Takada and Emanuel Ungaro, among others, bought half a hillside acre topped by a simple stucco house in rural Saint-Prix, 10 miles north of Paris, which has become his "garden of experiences."

The first night there, more than a decade ago, Risser discovered that he wasn't far enough from the city, because the pulsating light from the Eiffel Tower could reach his bedroom window. So he set about creating different arboreal tableaux—Versailles' *bosquets* gone

BELOW: Trees, including Japanese maples and a showy *Cornus contro-versa,* along the grassy path that opens onto a clearing beside the house also block out neighboring buildings and orchards from view.
RIGHT: The once prominent house is wood clad and less visible.
OVERLEAF: A curtain of *Phyllostachys viridiglaucescens* bamboo and a giant ladder chair facing views of Paris.

wild—to make his setting more country-like.

He clad the house with weathered pine planks, dug a rectangular swimming pool and began to plant away.

From the main road, a paved path now wends up through a jungle of Japanese maples and other trees to a manicured clearing of grass, where a showy white *Cornus controversa* announces the peaked, two-story home, and a potager beside it. However, they are hidden behind a magical see-through screen of 30-foot-tall *Phyllostachys viridiglaucescens* bamboo, whose lower stalks are stripped clean to let light in. The rectangular swimming pool bordered by tulips, muscari, fragrant narcissus, snowflakes, scilla, lilies, aliums, grasses and fig trees looks like a natural watering hole that fish and an air pump keep algae-free.

An old oak beside the pool supports a tree house with a grandstand view of this jungle, which is a laboratory for testing the versatility and adaptability of plants and vines Risser finds and then propagates for city clients.

PREVIOUS OVERLEAF: Risser's favorite *bosquet*—seen through a latticed gazebo—is a storybook copse of flowering *Ligustrum sinense*, deutzia and *Ilex castaneifolia* complemented with shale shards, aliums, poppies, white *Salix* 'Hakuro Nishiki', as well as hobbit furniture.
LEFT: Risser's tree house and pool blend into the foliage.
BELOW: Seats made from tree roots, like the pool raft, are artfully scattered throughout the garden.

Poolside Roof Garden

A Miami-esque sundeck rises on Rue Lecourbe

In Paris's Hauts-de-Seine environs, a narrow V-shaped deck hugging a triangular 11th-floor penthouse clad in corrugated aluminum had little to offer except a giant wood-clad concrete box of a swimming pool on its broader 16-foot-wide south side. However, its undeniable asset—a spectacular view of the Eiffel Tower, La Défense and all of Paris—made it ideal for outdoor living.

Enter Parisian landscape architect Christian Fournet, who specializes in pragmatic yet elegant gardens in tight spaces, and before long he designed a series of rooms for his clients, all connected by a white marble gravel and wood deck that adds instant warmth to the terrace.

"Small spaces can inspire great ideas because they make you think harder," Fournet said. "This terrace is all about a deck and its links to the sky, water and view."

To take better advantage of the vistas, the narrower eight-foot-wide section of the terrace steps up to a cozy landing for corner seating in the crook of the V-shaped deck. Another step up toward the pool on the other side makes the deck perfectly level with the top of the pool, and also provides room for two deck chaises with grandstand views of the city. A panel on the outer edge of the pool that prevents water from splashing over is of clear tempered glass to look through. Exterior metal railings have all been raised to correspond with the new deck heights, and deliberately untamed star jasmine interrupts the severity of their lines. Concealed lighting under treads makes walking safe at night.

Three steps down and a narrow corridor between the penthouse wall and the pool leads to a dining salon under a shade umbrella at the far end, which can also be accessed through French doors from inside the living space. At both ends of the V-shaped deck and along the exterior railings, Fournet installed an enfilade of rectangular pots made of zinc-colored resin that echoes the galvanized metal cladding. The purple, pink and red kalmias, camellias, crepe myrtles and abelia shrubs growing in these pots harmonize with the wood, and the varied heights of the containers echo the skyline.

The rhythmically interrupted wood decking makes the two sides of the terrace seem less long and narrow, and, quite unexpectedly, on a sunny day its contrasting weathered gray color makes the pool look as azure as the water in Miami's South Beach.

FACING AND RIGHT: A view of the Eiffel Tower and Paris inspired Christian Fournet's outdoor rooms and wood deck for a terrace with a raised pool that once seemed awkward in the small space.

Miniature Estate in Suresnes

Versailles redux in a suburban garden

ABOVE: The three-story red brick house has views of the garden.
FACING: The texturally rich, mainly green and white garden is planted, starting from the bottom tier, with flowers in beds, shrubs and then tall trees that blur the boundary and provide privacy.
OVERLEAF: The central tier, inspired by Japanese Zen sand gardens, is bordered by perennial euphorbias, as well as Mediterranean evergreens that are easy to maintain year-round.

In Suresnes, a suburb just west of Paris, landscape architect Christian Fournet emulated Le Nôtre's *jardins à la française* with rule-breaking fillips all his own.

The long, narrow, much-neglected 3,000-square-foot rectangular back garden he redesigned belonged to a couple that loved dining outdoors, but mainly wanted a pleasing area to look at from their three-story red brick home. Despite its sloped terrain, previous owners had installed a hard-to-get-to sitting area halfway up the garden that, in the winter, simply looked ugly and bare.

Using the existing three-tiered armature of the garden, Fournet created three outdoor rooms that are as varied as the *bosquets* at Versailles, but, linked by a central spine of undressed slate stairs and revealed in enfilade rather than concealed behind *palissades,* they offer a longer, visually exciting perspective.

To make each tier distinctive, Fournet used a variety of materials. Square terra-cotta tiles pave a dining patio at the lowest point next to the house. In the middle tier, white gravel covers a Zen court that has a square stone fountain at its center, and vertical slate slabs installed at each corner double as planters as well as retaining walls. The rectangular tier up top is covered with a keyhole-shaped lawn that disappears uphill into a thicket of trees that, like those at Vaux-le-Vicomte, give the impression of an endless garden.

"By erasing boundaries, you can make any garden seem limitless," Fournet explained. Moreover, because there is no obvious fence except for a low semicircular hedge at the top of the lawn and vertical slabs of slate surrounding the gravel garden, these trees offer privacy from neighbors.

Fournet, who counts fashion designers such as Emanuel Ungaro among his clients, also likes to play with texture, form and color. Sculptural balls of clipped boxwood in the slate planters form perennial textural bridges and frames for flowering shrubs such as wiry, narrow-leaved *Phillyrea angustifolia* contrasted with flowering dogwood *Cornus kousa* on three sides. These free-form, asymmetrically arranged additions ably counter the scourge of monotonous symmetry. And while evergreen species ensure a permanent presence of white and green in the garden, tropical clerodendrums, hibiscus shrubs, hydrangeas, berry blossoms and a beautiful Japanese maple, *Acer palmatum* 'Sangokaku', that turns to rich, vibrant orange-red in the fall all announce the seasons in turn.

A Private Key to Parc Monceau

Christian Fournet's small garden for a *hôtel particulier*

Ordinary Parisians had little access to aristocratic gardens such as the theatrical 1778 *Anglo-Chinois* Parc Monceau until it was purchased by the city and halved in 1860 by Baron Haussmann to make room for private townhouses during the Second Empire. That's when some of the shrunken-but-still-grand 8th arrondissement public garden's new neighbors got all-hours access to Monceau's 20 acres as if they were their own. For this Haussmann-era townhouse's gravel-covered back garden, landscape architect Christian Fournet added showy white hydrangeas, and within clipped boxwood borders, shaped to reflect architectural bays, he introduced Japanese maples, pink *Clerodendrum bungei* and texturally rich, large- and small-leaved, easy-care shrubs. After all, abundant trees, garden paths and follies lie just beyond its secret gate to Parc Monceau.

LEFT AND BELOW: Only a historic wrought iron fence with a discreet gate separates this 1860s townhouse garden from Parc Monceau.

205

Public Parks

Gardens are poems
Where you stroll with your hands in your pockets.
Pierre Albert-Birot

Parc Monceau's Illusory Past

All times and all places in one garden

Jardins Anglo-Chinois—English-style gardens with Chinese follies framed by trees—were popular among French aristocrats during the 1770s when Anglophile Louis Philippe Joseph d'Orléans, Duke of Chartres, added a free-form garden called Folie de Chartres around his formal estate in what is now Paris's 8th arrondissement.

The garden, later expanded and named after nearby Monceau village, was designed in 1778 by artist and writer Louis Carrogis Carmontelle to include varied structures and plants that "unite, in one garden, all times and all places." Carmontelle and architect Bernard Poyet added operatic "scenes" within this picturesque geographical, historical and natural fiction, preferring set-like illusions in gardens with liveried attendants to the somber melancholia of true English landscapes.

Nonetheless, in 1781 Scottish gardener Thomas Blaikie added hushed English woods and lawns, and in 1787 when a city toll barrier closed off the park's northern edge, the duke commissioned Claude Nicolas Ledoux to design a customs house that resembled a circular classical temple. The barrier fell during the French Revolution but the rotunda, or Pavillon de Chartres, remains.

The duke was guillotined in 1793, but his garden, halved to about 20 acres during Napoleon III's reign when it was subdivided for town houses, survived. In 1860 it opened as Parc Monceau after Baron Haussmann added two wide carriageways. Curving paths for strolling, showy Oriental plane trees, a grotto and waterfalls were also added, and architect Gabriel Davioud designed baroque cast iron fencing and capped the rotunda with a dome. His Venetian bridge replaced Carmontelle's exotic Chinese footbridge over a stream.

A Roman colonnade around a large oval lily pond and a miniature Egyptian pyramid in the Wood of Tombs are Carmontelle's originals. They help us imagine his vanished Chinese gate, Tartar tent, farmhouse, Dutch windmill, Temple of Mars, minaret, Italian vineyard, grotto, and "a Gothic building serving as a chemistry laboratory." In their stead, statues of nineteenth-century writers and musicians, including Guy de Maupassant and Chopin, now fittingly dot this storied park conceived by a dramatist.

LEFT, TOP: Carmontelle's 1778 Corinthian colonnade around his oval lake.
LEFT: Davioud's 1860s bridge inspired by Venice's Rialto.
FACING: A grotto and waterfall added during the Second Empire.
OVERLEAF, LEFT: Cascading golden chain (*Laburnum anagyroides*) flowers.
OVERLEAF, RIGHT: Carmontelle's miniature 1778 Egyptian pyramid.

A Living Archive of the Planet

Albert Kahn's gardens of the world

While many Paris parks are textbook French, the Albert Kahn Museum and Garden is a tapestry of international garden styles and a window to the world.

Spread over 10 acres in the Paris suburb of Boulogne-Billancourt, this horticultural wonderland surrounds the former home of Albert Kahn, an Alsatian-born financier, humanitarian and pacifist who recommended a deeper understanding of world culture.

To that end, Kahn's vast garden was planted from 1896 to 1902 with species from many countries to form a tapestry of gardens. A domed glass and steel greenhouse housed tropical plants, while several miniature forests, including full-grown conifers with wildflowers below them like those in the Vosges Mountains of Alsace, sections of prairieland and rocky terrain, a rose garden, a formal French garden and a picturesque English garden had as their centerpiece an asymmetrical Japanese garden comprising a colorful, sloping garden and a quiet teahouse. There, key figures in the arts and sciences, including Rabindranath Tagore, Colette, Albert Einstein and Rodin, conferred at Kahn's invitation.

From 1909 until the financial crash of the 1930s, Kahn also commissioned 72,000 photographs and countless movies of far-flung people whose ways were threatened by war and modernity. They were preserved after his death in 1940, and a new museum by architect Kengo Kuma will better showcase them.

Restored by the Département des Hauts-de-Seine after years of neglect, the Kahn garden thrives again as a public park near the Seine, evoking foreign lands. In a section of the new Japanese garden by landscape architect Fumiaki Takano, which replaced the original, hills and a pond suggest the presence of mountains and seas, and trimmed mounds of carmine and fuchsia azaleas form hillocks while irises spring up under Japanese maples, magnolias and cherry trees. Elsewhere, cedars and Norway spruce form a cool blue "forest," underplanted with hostas and hydrangeas, and black pines, moss-covered boulders and rough forest paths lead to the soft grasses of an English garden, which in turn is separated by a serpentine rivulet from manicured French gardens bordered by a simple gravel path.

FACING AND RIGHT: In a stream and pond are green lily pads, and in the air the scent of jasmine. Steep, pebbly paths, bamboo railings, orange koi, stepping stones in the water and a bright red drum bridge, inspired by the Sacred Bridge of Nikko, all evoke Japan.

FACING AND ABOVE: Transitions between the various botanical sections at the Albert Kahn Garden are obvious. A rustic footbridge leads into a gnarled grotto in the northeast corner. Farther west, in a level rose garden, deep pink ramblers arbored every few feet above a neat grid of wide footpaths and strips of lawn with other red rose varieties and espaliered apples and quince share space.

Uncommon Sculpture Park

A cemetery garden praises the dead

Père Lachaise cemetery in Paris's 20th arrondissement, named after the seventeenth-century Jesuit advisor to Louis XIV, Père François de La Chaise, is where the likes of Irish writer Oscar Wilde lie alongside a million other famous and lesser-known people, making the verdant 114-acre graveyard one of the largest troves of the world's greatest talents—albeit six feet under.

For the millions who come to pay homage to these stars each year, Père Lachaise, founded in 1804 by Napoleon Bonaparte, is also an open-air museum of 69,000 ostentatious tombs and monuments fashioned by artists and architects such as Henri Chapu, David

LEFT AND BELOW: Père Lachaise cemetery's planted islands and parks are linked by winding cobbled streets rather than a grid of paths.
OVERLEAF: The beautiful 1899 Aux Morts monument to the dead by Paul-Albert Bartholomé also conceals an ossuary for the disinterred.

d'Angers, Charles Garnier, Hector Guimard and Louis Visconti from the nineteenth century until now. An elaborate Neo-Byzantine columbarium by Jean-Camille Formigé added in 1894 is another magnet.

Laid out like a city rather than a typical cemetery, with long avenues and winding circular streets that connect "neighborhoods," Père Lachaise was designed by architect Alexandre-Théodore Brongniart, who is also buried there. It is an unusual walled town on a hill that people can enter through one of five gates during the day and must leave before dark.

The most impressive gate, by Neoclassical architect Étienne-Hippolyte Godde, who also designed the 1823 funerary chapel on the site where the Jesuits once lived, leads to an almost secret 1899 ossuary carefully hidden behind the Aux Morts ("To the Dead") monument by Paul-Albert Bartholomé.

Some visitors come with picnic baskets (although there are almost no places left on the ground to sit) to call on writer Colette, composer Chopin, writer Honoré de Balzac, singer Édith Piaf, dancer Isadora Duncan or singer Jim Morrison of the Doors. Add American author Gertrude Stein, Indian aviator J. R. D. Tata, glass sculptor René Lalique, painters Jean Ingres and Max Ernst and soprano Maria Callas to the list and you still only have a tip of history's celebrity iceberg. Evidently, for permanent entrée to this popular secular cemetery-cum-sculpture garden for the elite that had to be expanded five times in 50 years, you only have to have lived or died in Paris as they did.

Against a section of a rough stone wall now called the Communards' or Federalists' Wall, 147 members of the Paris Commune, some of whom had torched the Tuileries Palace, and defenders of nearby Belleville were shot for insurrection in 1871 on Père Lachaise's grounds, and they are ignominiously buried there in an unmarked grave. Bullet holes identify the spot, and ivy and begonias cover the earth where they fell.

For the others at Père Lachaise whose names we do know from simple graves and tombstones or ornate sepulchers decorated with statuary, gilt-framed pictures, priceless Sèvres vases, stained glass windows and bronze doors, and tributes of real or fake porcelain or painted metal flowers—this quiet retreat roamed by cats under the shade of old lime and chestnut trees that belong in a quiet English garden is a kind of crowded urban heaven.

LEFT AND FACING: Faded metal tole and porcelain floral decorations on moss-covered graves are tenacious reminders in every season of flowers Parisians love in life and, it is assumed, in death.

Fondation Cartier's Botanical Theater

The nature of things in a gallery garden

The Fondation Cartier pour l'Art Contemporain began showcasing contemporary art in a sylvan suburban landscape when it was founded in 1984. No surprise, then, that when its headquarters moved in 1994 from Jouy-en-Josas, near Versailles, into an airy, Jean Nouvel–designed, seven-story, steel-and-glass building on busy Boulevard Raspail in central Paris, it was complemented by a modern garden.

The new garden, near the nineteenth-century cemetery of Montparnasse in the 14th arrondissement, is also a sculpture park—or rather a sculptural work itself—created by German conceptual artist Lothar Baumgarten, who calls it Theatrum Botanicum, referring to medieval books in which monks inventoried native medicinal and aromatic plants growing in their gardens.

In this case, it is the books coming alive. Although there are some herbal plants like vervain in Theatrum Botanicum, Baumgarten's 35 different species of commonly found local trees, shrubs, wildflowers and weeds were all chosen to multiply untended over time. He wanted to observe a landscape that becomes "a living space" when it is naturally seeded.

Some call his park "wild" and that is exactly how Baumgarten envisioned it. There are no "Do not walk on the grass" signs here because most of the grasses will easily surface again. However, if the garden is a facsimile of untamed nature, it is also tuned to the seasons. Its more than 200 types of plants include wild strawberries that appear at the same time as fruit on fig trees. Its wild violets coincide with lily of the valley, and mint and rosemary plants flourish when cherries start to ripen. Some of Baumgarten's original plantings survive, and others reintroduced in 2005 include rare species or ones that are beginning to disappear in the region, like columbine (*Aquilegia vulgaris*), monkshood (*Aconitum napellus*), sneezewort (*Achillea ptarmica*), yellow foxglove (*Digitalis lutea*) and leafy spurge (*Euphorbia esula*).

Although the triangular garden is inspired obliquely by introverted medieval walled gardens, the new design has unique features that link it to its contemporary locale. For instance, its 40-foot-high front wall, like the transparent, reflective building the garden surrounds, is made of glass panels and steel. This unusually high "garden wall" is nearly as tall as a magnificent cedar of Lebanon in front of the main entrance, planted there in 1823 by the property's former aristocratic resident, nineteenth-century writer François-René de Chateaubriand. The

FACING: Conceptual artist Lothar Baumgarten's informal terraced amphitheater garden called Theatrum Botanicum is deliberately "wild."
ABOVE: A sandy path wends around the steel-and-glass Fondation Cartier building by Jean Nouvel to the back garden amphitheater.

223

glass screen helps to shield the historic tree from winds, and the garden from ambient traffic sounds, yet puts them in full view of the street. The ground-floor gallery, which has tall sliding glass panels, opens to the gently sloped back garden, which is shored by sweeping concrete arcs that form wide grassy terraces. In this informal amphitheater people sit or gather during concerts and outdoor presentations. Off to one side, an elliptical sunken terrace paved with French limestone has a built-in contemplation bench, and meandering gravel walkways are arranged along Chateaubriand's vestigial paths within the garden.

At Jouy-en-Josas, the Fondation's expansive grounds were clearly outdoor galleries. In the city, its roughly one-acre garden is a gallery, but it is also a petri dish of ideas that can be cross-pollinated.

In 1992, Italian sculptor Giuseppe Penone, whose recent retrospective at Versailles coincided with the 400th anniversary of Le Nôtre's birth, had created a bronze tree limb called *Biforcazione* for Jouy-en-Josas, but it was moved to the new Boulevard Raspail garden in Paris where it lies lifeless, seemingly discarded on the ground. Yet a fountain of water trickling from a gash in its gnarled weathered elbow provides Baumgarten with a perfect metaphor for seasonal cycles and rebirth in his conceptual garden.

For a 1998 exhibition called Être Nature (Being Nature), Patrick Blanc installed one of his first vertical gardens above the entrance to Nouvel's building, where it remains—fed only by circulating drips of nutrient-rich water—as proof of Blanc's theory that that is all cliff-hugging plants need.

Long after it was installed, Baumgarten's urban wilderness has also developed the ecosystem he had hoped for. Theatrum Botanicum encourages small creatures, birds and beetles that thrive only in such native habitats but also help to seed it. Insectivores live in the garden, signaling its rich diversity to more birds from neighboring parks and the cemetery nearby. Even sparrows find as safe a haven there as the endangered European Michaelmas daisy (*Aster amellus*), and butterflies, especially the ivy-loving holly blue butterfly, have made it home.

Nature, it seems, is just being Nature.

LEFT, TOP: Steel braces tie the garden's tall glass fence to the building. In the foreground is Chateaubriand's ancient cedar of Lebanon.
LEFT: Detail of Giuseppe Penone's 1992 bronze *Biforcazione* fountain that explores the artist's fascination with transience.
FACING: Patrick Blanc's thriving 1998 *mur vegetal* and the majestic, historic cedar of Lebanon, also reflected in the glass façade, are emblems of continuity.

Gilles Clément's Steamy Jungle

Tropical wonders at the Musée du Quai Branly

A colorful building for the ethnographic Musée du Quai Branly, designed by architect Jean Nouvel as part of Paris's Grands Projets, stands in the center of a gently undulating site in central Paris that was carefully sculpted into protective berms to keep the Seine, should it ever flood, at bay.

But the elongated polygonal east–west structure, completed in 2006 and held aloft on 33-foot-high *piloti*, or columns, of varying thicknesses that allude to stilts or totem poles, is engulfed instead by a "wild" garden of bamboo, shrubs, ferns and Asian miscanthus. The renowned landscape designer Gilles Clément, who also codesigned the avant-garde Parc André Citroën, created this atypical garden with what he calls a "planetary intermixture" of 30 plant species from different biomes because he did not want "a heavily cultivated, occidental landscape." Drawing on first-hand experiences as a young man in Africa, where he also discovered the rare *Bunoeopsis clementii* butterfly in the Republic of Cameroon in 1974, Clément has developed ideas not often seen in public parks. As a self-proclaimed "gardener," who is also among France's most venerated theorists at the Versailles National School of Landscape Architecture, Clément selected more than 170 trees, including oaks from Europe, maples from America, and magnolias and cherry trees from Japan, for his "world garden."

Narrow garden paths and meandering walkways of stone, gravel and concrete that seem to ebb and flow under and around the building like a river link all sections of the fluid public space that is intended to reflect the museum's global artifacts inspired by animism and nature. To add to this conceit, Clément has randomly embedded tortoise-shaped artifacts, conch shells and other tribal motifs in clear acrylic capsules within the park.

Leaving all such obvious cultural references aside, Clément, who is an ardent ecologist, explained to an audience of students that he is also interested in protecting

FACING: Bamboo, Asian miscanthus and trees frame the Musée du Quai Branly building designed by architect Jean Nouvel.

RIGHT, TOP: A skylit concrete pavilion with a green roof, built-in banquettes and tables for children's art classes and other activities.

RIGHT: Sacred flowers, insects and shells under discs of clear plastic are embedded in walkways that link the north and south gardens along the length of the colorful polygonal building.

OVERLEAF: Details of gramineaes and ferns with LED and plexiglass reeds by artist Yann Kersalé that light up eerily at night.

natural diversity of many kinds. He believes that even weeds that appear annually can keep a garden fresh and "in movement." That's why Quai Branly's wooded thicket is also "a sort of savanna with a lot of gramineaes and flowers" that can reseed at will. Certain sections of the garden willingly accept vagabond plants that inevitably crop up along pathways and in garden beds thanks to birds and other creatures that inhabit this piece of "wilderness" amid nineteenth-century Haussmannian buildings in the 7th arrondissement.

Several other design strategies help to keep Clément's four-and-a-half-acre Parisian garden worlds away. For instance, Nouvel's 40-foot-high and 660-foot-wide glass fence—not dissimilar to the one he designed for the Fondation Cartier a decade earlier—acts as a barrier to muffle traffic sounds along the garden's busy northern edge on the quay. Inside the garden, the rumble of cars quickly gives way to the soothing sound of birds and sometimes ethnic music floating up from a sunken amphitheater within the jungle landscape. In the south section of the garden, there is an estuarine water feature on whose southern boundary a resin-covered steel fence designed to simulate reeds keeps people out after hours, but not bracken or self-seeding nomadic grasses that soften the edge.

While most of the garden unfolds gradually like a fable, one ever-visible and instantly recognizable feature is a vertical garden by Clément's fellow botanist and famed *mur vegetal* designer Patrick Blanc that clads the curved north façade of the museum's four-story administration wing facing the Seine. It redefines the meaning and purpose of the traditional "garden wall" but also echoes Clément's choices of flora from the places where the museum's collection originates: Asia, Africa, Oceania and the Americas. Blanc's selections of 150 tropical plant species have taken root on felt tacked to his wall that is drip irrigated from the top with runoff water that is collected in a gutter at the bottom and re-circulated periodically. Because the wall is curved, Blanc has discovered that his north-facing plants have to be hardier than the ones facing east, and like an artist, he too continues to perfect his canvas of 15,000 plants for birds and lizards who call this "world garden" in the shadow of the Eiffel Tower home.

FACING: Patrick Blanc's four-story-high tropical *mur vegetal* on the museum's building on Quai Branly sports bergenias, pachysandras and heucheras, as well as ferns, sedges, mosses and liverworts.
RIGHT, TOP: The rear section of the vertical garden.
RIGHT: On the south boundary, "reeds" of resin-coated steel form a pervious but secure enclosure that blends in with estuarine foliage.

When Plants Make Waves

Louis Benech's nautical rooftop fantasy

When Sébastien Charléty Stadium was built by former merchant seaman and architect Henri Gaudin in 1994, its car park's flat, segment-shaped roof—wedged between the stadium and the Cimetière de Chantilly—proved ideal for a watery conceit by Paris *paysagiste* Louis Benech.

Dubbed Square Jean-Claude Nicolas Forestier, the one-and-a-half-acre garden honors Napoleon III's superintendent of public parks, whose mentor, Jean-Charles Alphand, reconfigured Parc Monceau. Like Forestier, who famously transformed the Champ-de-Mars into a congenial public park, Benech is also known for combining nineteenth-century-style French formality with loose naturalism—traits amply displayed here. In the classic mode, the park is planted with a luxurious, gently undulating lawn in the center "for sun and sky." However, clipped dogwood (*Cornus mas*) hedges around

LEFT AND BELOW: A row of undulating, clipped dogwood hedges, far left, and a naturalistic thicket of trees and swirling beds border a central lawn skirted by a gravel-covered walking path.
OVERLEAF: Pink valerians, irises and foamy white flowers against dark holm oaks, strawberry trees (*Arbutus unedo*), a clipped ball of green olive (*Phillyrea latifolia*) and willow-leaved pear (*Pyrus salicifolia*).

a children's section have softly rolling tops, and, in beds surrounding the lawn, expressionistic massings of seaside and Mediterranean species such as cistus, euphorbia, lavender, santolina and arbutus all allude to sea spray and waves as a nod to Gaudin's days on the high seas.

The northeast and west sides of the park contain 179 trees, such as holm oaks, a sound-muffling cork oak, silver-leaved *Pyrus nivalis,* a white *Salix alba* willow, and a fig tree, in lieu of trees felled during the building's construction that had to be replaced by law. With mature evergreen and deciduous trees forming a filigreed canopy, views of the cemetery are obscured, and on the north edge the trees blend in with purple-leafed street trees. Paths cut through the restful, scenic woods and circle the boat-shaped lawn, which is lined with more eddies of foamy white flowers and silver foliage, such as *Rhodotypos scandens,* "Iceberg" and "Nevada" roses, *Rosa fedtschenkoana, Viburnum plicatum* 'Watanabe', as well as valerians and purple irises for a burst of color.

BELOW: A triangular bed eddying into the lawn near the children's section is reserved for annuals such as salvias, purpletop vervain (*Verbena bonariensis*) and golden-yellow rudbeckia.

RIGHT: White gaura (*Gaura lindheimeri*) and trees such as ubame oak (*Quercus phillyraeoides*) simulate crashing waves and sea foam.

A New Leaf for the Archives

Centuries-old gardens revived by Louis Benech

In the Marais, four enclosed classic French and *Anglo-Chinois* back gardens with shared boundaries were kept hidden for centuries. The 3rd arrondissement gems belonged to the Hôtel de Soubise, the Hôtel de Rohan and four other mansions on Rue des Francs-Bourgeois that held the Archives Nationales since 1808, but only recently were the gardens made public.

In 1667, Marie de Guise, mistress to Louis XIV, recruited André Le Nôtre for one garden, and in 1700, her manse, renamed Hôtel de Soubise by its new owner François de Rohan, prince of Soubise, was remodeled with ovoid garden-facing salons and a Baroque façade, with allegorical sculptures of the seasons. These aristocrats and their neighbors vanished, but their gardens remained, suffering neglect and visual encroachments.

Landscape designer Louis Benech, who worked on the Tuileries Garden during the 1990s, came to the rescue.

Combining and refining "the existing gardens of various old houses into one huge one-and-a-half-acre public space" required simple touches, Benech said. He added informal swaths of wildflower "meadows" between conical yew topiaries in the cobbled *cour d'honneur* entry. The hidden, picturesque Second Empire gardens

LEFT AND BELOW: The Hôtel de Soubise *cour d'honneur*. A northeast gate (seen below left) leads to hidden interior gardens.

of the Hôtel d'Assy and Hôtel de Fontenay, and the symmetrical gardens of the Hôtel de Jaucourt and Hôtel de Rohan are all linked by an *allée*—Rue de la Roche—of pollarded plane trees, which he only nudged higher to block modern buildings from view.

Roses cluttering the d'Assy and de Fontenay gardens were removed to make an existing "river" and pond, with curving walking paths and large trees, including one of Paris's rare Indian horse chestnuts dominating the conjoined gardens, the foci. "Open space is also more important than hard-to-maintain clipped borders," Benech said. So simplified lawns were softened with hydrangeas, fragrant sarcococcas and lilacs at the edges that "belong to the period of the buildings."

The de Jaucourt garden now has flowering crabapple and cherry trees, and the de Rohan garden with central turf *parterres à l'anglaise* was sparked with tussock grass (*Deschampsia cespitosa*) in wire cages to echo stables nearby.

"It wasn't about coming up with something new, but about being inspired by what was 'written,'" Benech said.

FACING: The boundary of the de Fontenay and de Jaucourt gardens.
ABOVE: Rue de la Roche, seen from the de Rohan garden, has a raised hedge and pollarded plane trees bordering it.
RIGHT: In the d'Assy garden's river pond, Benech restored a nineteenth-century-style rockery with fringed irises and daylillies.

The New Metro Style

Outdoor art for the masses

Sculpture has been a part of Parisian gardens for centuries. Indeed, the city's public realm—reshaped during the 1850s by Baron Haussmann—can be viewed as one large, art-filled garden. Since 1900, the most iconic sculptural features of Paris were clearly architect Hector Guimard's plant-inspired Art Nouveau *métro* entrances of cast iron, bronze and glass. That was until 2000, when conceptual artist Jean-Michel Othoniel's delightful double-domed canopy for the Palais Royal subway entrance called *Kiosque des Noctambules* (Kiosk of the Nightwalkers) rose as rival.

Fittingly, pedestrians use Othoniel's kiosk on small, tree-lined Place Colette, close to the Comédie Française, well into the night. Composed of six columns made of signature Murano blown-glass globes and brushed aluminum balls threaded together like rosaries that hold up the domes, and a filigreed aluminum railing and bench inset with colored glass disks, the fragile-looking yet solid entrance has survived many a traveler and night owl. Yet few know that Othoniel's canopy resembling a carriage in a charming fairy tale or a pair of royal crowns is also vested with symbols of time, transition and longing.

Its domes, each with a colored Venetian glass statuette finial from Salviati, rub up against each other to form a figure eight representing eternity, and their warm and cool palettes suggest the colors of day and night. The voluptuous glass globes allude to jewelry and echo recurring Othoniel themes surrounding the body, beauty and desire. Time is kinder to objects we love than to people who simply disappear into voids, the artist suggests. Inside the station, Othoniel refers to a lost grotto created for Catherine de Medici. Embedded in its walls are more globes in clear glass cisterns. These, as well as colored glass medallions or coins set into the subway stairs and railings, symbolize treasures people cast into wells and fountains for luck. Othoniel has clearly been lucky, judging by a 2011 French postage stamp honoring his kiosk. But the best fortune is that the delicate work has been accepted with love, not vandalism.

LEFT AND FACING: Jean-Michel Othoniel's *Kiosque des Noctambules*. Its murano glass components cast colored shadows by day, and in lamplight, aluminum "beads" gleam at night.
OVERLEAF, LEFT: More street art in a Louis Vuitton store window.
OVERLEAF, RIGHT: Artful riveted steel and masonry underpinnings of an elevated railway line that belongs to a post-Haussmann Paris.

Lofty Promenade Plantée

A trail of green near the Bastille

Paris, the *Ville Lumière* of Louis XIV with its cafes, well-lit streets and spectacular gardens, was long the envy of other cities. It had set the standard for European modernity well before Napoleon III's prefect of the Seine, Baron Haussmann, added wide avenues and transformed royal hunting grounds into the enormous, picturesque Bois de Vincennes public park. About a century and a half later, in the same *arrondissement* as the famous nineteenth-century park, Paris unveiled the world's first elevated garden on an abandoned railway viaduct in 1993, and even American cities followed.

However, Paris's avant-garde Promenade Plantée, or Coulée Verte (French for Planted Walkway, or Green Corridor), by landscape architect Jacques Vergely and architect Philippe Mathieux, wasn't much noticed for nearly two decades. Perhaps that's because the narrow greenbelt the designers created atop the 1859 red brick Vincennes Railway viaduct on Avenue Daumesnil, just east of Place de la Bastille, was less in step with the zeitgeist of the 1980s, during which President François Mitterrand's grand architectural projects created an appetite for the grandiose, shiny and the new. This unusually modest, leafy urban park reflecting conservation, simplicity and utility simply did not make waves when it opened, unlike New York City's celebrated High Line Park on an elevated 1930s freight rail line when it was first unveiled in 2009. Obviously, repurposing such abandoned public structures has only now become the preferred norm.

When the City of Paris finally chose to radically transform the long unused stations and tracks of the Vincennes steam railway that went from Bastille to Verneuil-l'Ètang through Vincennes until 1969, it was in large part to revitalize the forgotten neighborhood. But it knew that just a quiet park could not achieve that and so it replaced the railway's western-most station at Place de la Bastille with the ambitious Opéra Bastille by Carlos Ott in 1989. Other stations or depots along the next three miles of the century-old route were converted into large squares and parks, all linked together by the slender Promenade. The walkway incorporated the

FACING: The Promenade Plantée park high atop a defunct viaduct.
RIGHT, TOP: The red brick arcades of the Viaduc des Arts, a row of new shops and cafes. The tree-lined raised promenade is visible.
RIGHT: Steel sections of the viaduct reflect the French penchant for Egyptian-style columns and obelisks during the Empire periods.

historic arcaded viaduct in the first half of the route, as well as ground-level trenches and tunnels farther east toward the Boulevard Périphérique, and close to the old Porte Dorée and the Bois de Vincennes.

As an artery of progress, composed of wood, gravel and paving in place of the old rail tracks, the Promenade was also ahead of the naturalism trend in landscape design, and Vergely and Mathieux encouraged native grasses growing spontaneously on the sides of the central path meant for runners and pedestrians. Carefully cultivated flower beds, potted lime and hazelnut trees, reflecting ponds, climbing roses and vines over arched, trellised sections for shade, and park benches completed their design.

The Promenade links together the Square Hector Malot, the Jardin de la Gare de Reuilly (where the old station building is preserved), the Square Charles Péguy and the largest park, which is at the halfway point and at the foot of the viaduct's eastern end, the Jardin de Reuilly-Paul Pernin. Architect Pierre Colboc with the Groupe Paysages designed this park in 1992. At its Avenue Daumesnil entrance is the first public fountain in France that offers still *and* sparkling water. The Jardin de Reuilly is also a delightful mélange of theme gardens that have terraced garden walls, trees such as hackberry and maples with green and white striated bark, perennial flower beds, bamboo, ferns, euphorbias, heather, sedums and roses, as well as a giant semicircular picnic meadow over which a footbridge arcs gracefully from the old viaduct to Allée Vivaldi and the lower stretches of the Promenade where bicyclists can roam.

With the opening of the Opéra Bastille, and with the transformation of the 71 empty arcades of the viaduct by Patrick Berger and Jean-Michel Wilmotte into a long row of tony art and craft boutiques and cafes, all collectively referred to as the Viaduc des Arts, the city succeeded in bringing commerce to the streets. But the nearly three-story-high Promenade, accessible by stairs and elevators, which in some stretches cuts through modern buildings that have risen around it, has brought an unexpected thrill: voyeuristic views of Paris life.

TOP, LEFT: A cocoon of grasses, vines, trees and Mediterranean shrubs.
LEFT: The elevated promenade intersects with the Jardin de Reuilly-Paul Pernin's several themed gardens on the site of a former rail depot, including this one with a female nude by Raymond Delamarre titled *For Oppressed People*. Also visible is the spire of the 12th arrondissement 1876 town hall designed by Antoine-Julien Hénard.
FACING: Stairs from the Promenade skirt a wall garden by architect Pierre Colboc and Groupe Paysages, who created Jardin de Reuilly.

A Dockside Landscape

A rooftop public park by Jakob + MacFarlane

A 1907 warehouse by Georges Morin-Goustiaux on Quai d'Austerlitz was perhaps Paris's first reinforced concrete structure, yet "the city considered demolishing it to make a place for a park," modern architect Brendan MacFarlane said. Instead, in 2008, his Paris firm Jakob + MacFarlane transformed the four-story, 13th arrondissement structure into "a real and virtual landscape" called Les Docks—Cité de la Mode et du Design. It is a fashion and design hub with a school, gallery, shops and a 25,000-square-foot rooftop park with views of the Seine. A new arborescent, latticed cladding of green painted steel and fritted glass complementing the building's revealed concrete armature "grows from the old grid as new branches grow on a tree," MacFarlane said. Up the building sides, the cladding swells out to make room for stairs and, on the roof, forms faceted pavilions for restaurants and clubs. To complete the "garden," Michel Desvigne planted sedums and grasses atop the shelters and within cutouts in the roof's French oak decking.

FACING AND BELOW: Restaurant pavilions with hardy green roofs in a new rooftop park above Les Docks on the river Seine.
OVERLEAF: Their painted steel entrances "look like open umbrellas on their sides," according to architect Brendan MacFarlane.

Novotel's Secret Courtyard

Christian Fournet's modern *parterre*

An interior courtyard and *salon de thé* designed by Christian Fournet at central Paris's recently remodeled U-shaped hotel Novotel Les Halles, is a little-known treasure that, like classic *parterres,* is enjoyed even from rooms up high, yet the plan allows for alcoves and islands of privacy. Its sinuous bands of slate and marble pavers, like sand in a Zen garden, contrast with the stiff building and swirl toward a rust-colored drainage ribbon. The seams, where stone and Cor-ten steel meet, cleverly let water through. Designed to look its best year-round, the garden sports a variety of evergreen flowering shrubs in a showy two-storied *mur vegetal* and also raised beds of cantilevered slate. They are accented by silvery hydrangeas, lilies, variegated Asian dogwood, medicinal camphor and fragrant Tibetan styrax, as well as showy foliage and an occasional burst of color.

LEFT AND BELOW: Novotel Les Halles's courtyard is enlivened with swirling bands of pavers, a rust-colored ribbon drain and banquettes.

Resources

The chief danger about Paris
is that it is such a strong stimulant.

— *T. S. Eliot*

Web Sites

Designers

AteliersMichaelHerrman.com
CamilleMuller.com
ChristianFournet.com
ErikBorja.fr
GillesClement.com
Hjardins.fr (Pierre-Alexandre Risser)
HuguesPeuvergne.fr
JakobMacfarlane.com
JeffLeatham.com
LouisBenech.com
Manuella-Editions.fr (Pascal Cribier)
NicolasGilsoul.com
PatrickJouin.com
VerticalGardenPatrickBlanc.com

Estates and Other Gardens

CiteModeDesign.fr
Courances.net
DesertdeRetz.info
En.ChateauVersailles.fr
Fondation.Cartier.com
FourSeasons.com/Paris
Giverny.org
MandarinOriental.com/Paris
Musee-Rodin.fr
Novotel.com/gb/hotel-0785-novotel-
  paris-les-halles/index.shtml
QuaiBranly.fr
Vaux-le-Vicomte.com

Plants, Pots and Stores

Arzinc.fr
Botanic.com
CultureIndoor.com
Delbard.fr
DelphineMessmerMosaique.com
DPI-France.com
Jardinez.com
JardinsJardin.com
LaBulberaie.fr
LArtDuJardin.com/en/
LOrangerie.fr
Ma-Pelouse.com
MoulieFleurs.com
JeanRey.fr
Poterie-Ravel.com
Saisons-Deco.com
StephaneOlivier.fr
VerteLigne.com
Vilmorin-Jardin.fr

PREVIOUS OVERLEAF AND FACING: *L'Instant Grand Siècle,* a conceptual vertical garden of 10,000 fragrant roses by designer Nicolas Gilsoul, sponsored by Laurent Perrier at Jardins, Jardin, an annual Paris garden show at the Tuileries cofounded by Pierre-Alexandre Risser along the lines of L'Art du Jardin at the Palais Royal by Aude de Thuin. ABOVE: One of 20 bronzes by Aristide Maillol donated by the sculptor's muse, Dina Vierny, and installed amid hedges radiating from the Arc de Triomphe du Carrousel between the Louvre and the Tuileries by André Malraux, French minister of culture in 1964.

Bibliography

Baverey, Michel, editor, *Pascal Cribier: Itinéraires d'un jardinier,* Xavier Barral, 2009.

Berrall, Julia S., *The Garden: An illustrated History,* Viking, 1966.

Boudassou, Bénédicte, *Les jardins de Christian Fournet,* printed privately, 2013.

Cahill, Susan, *Hidden Gardens of Paris: A Guide to the Parks, Squares, and Woodlands of the City of Light,* St. Martin's Griffin, 2012.

Chaufourier, Jean, with engravings by Jacques Rigaud, *The Gardens of Le Nôtre at Versailles,* Alain de Gourcuff, 2000.

Cox, Madison, *Private Gardens of Paris,* Harmony Books, 1989.

d'Arnoux, Alexandra, and Bruno de Laubadère, *The Secret Gardens of Paris,* Thames & Hudson, 2000.

————, *Terraces and Roof Gardens of Paris,* Flammarion, 2002.

de Saint Sauveur, Armelle, with photographs by Claire de Virieu, *Camille Muller: Les mains dans la terre,* Ulmer, 2012.

Gaillard, Marc, *Quais et ponts de Paris,* Éditions du Moniteur, 1982.

Hobhouse, Penelope, *The Story of Gardening,* DK, 2002.

Jansen, Eric, *Louis Benech: Twelve French Gardens,* Gourcuff Gradenigo, 2013.

Ketcham, Diana, *Le Désert de Retz: A Late Eighteenth-Century French Folly Garden, the Artful Landscape of Monsieur de Monville,* MIT Press, 1994.

Lablaude, Pierre-André, *Les jardins de Versailles,* Éditions Scala, 1995.

Laird, Mark, *The Formal Garden: Traditions of Art and Nature,* Thames & Hudson, 1992.

————, *The Flowering of the Landscape Garden: English Pleasure Grounds, 1720–1800,* University of Pennsylvania Press, 1999.

Le Dantec, Denise, and Jean-Pierre Le Dantec, *Reading the French Garden: Story and History,* MIT Press, 1993.

Le Page, Rosenn, *Les jardins à vivre de Pierre-Alexandre Risser: 25 ans de jardin à Paris et ailleurs,* Ulmer, 2011.

Orsenna, Érik, translated by Moishe Black, *André Le Nôtre: Gardener to the Sun King,* George Braziller, 2001.

Othoniel, Jean-Michel, *L'herbier merveilleux: Notes sur le sens caché des fleurs dans la peinture,* Actes Sud, 2008.

Peuvergne, Hugues, *Carnet de travail d'un jardinier paysagiste,* Ulmer, 2013.

Pizzoni, Filippo, translated by Judith Landry, *The Garden: A History in Landscape and Art,* Rizzoli, 1999.

Schlienger, Isabelle, *Splendeur des Jardins d'Île-de-France,* Flammarion, 1996.

Wiebenson, Dora, *The Picturesque Garden in France,* Princeton University Press, 1978.

FACING: Detail of the 1995 bronze fountain by Georges Jeanclos that depicts the life of Saint Julien le Pauvre at the rose-filled Square René Viviani on the Left Bank opposite Notre Dame Cathedral. This is also where, it is presumed, Paris's oldest tree, a false acacia (*Robinia pseudoacacia*), was planted in 1602 by botanist Jean Robin, the royal herbalist for kings Henry IV and Louis XIII.

Acknowledgments

We sincerely thank Gibbs Smith and all our friends in Paris, San Francisco, and elsewhere who opened doors to the many expressive gardens we've documented over a number of seasons. Our special thanks go to *Interiors* magazine editorial director Michael Wollaeger, former *Architectural Digest* Paris editor Alexandra d'Arnoux, landscape artist Shirley Watts, editor and garden writer Catherine Delvaux, architect Michael Herrman, filmmaker Gilles-Marie Tiné, multimedia artist Naomie Kremer, architect Anne Fougeron, art collector Robert Shimshak, Manuella Éditions editor Michel Baverey, landscape architect Louis Benech, Savannah College of Art and Design creative initiatives director Molly Rowe, Merchant Ivory Productions France co–managing director Gil Donaldson, Alexandre de Vogüé of Vaux-le-Vicomte, M-A-D designer Erik Adigard, couturier Martin Grant, Valentine Hansen de Ganay of Courances, Four Seasons Hôtel George V, the Mandarin Oriental Hotel, and luxury brand strategist Paul Burditch.

FACING: A copy of the legendary Farnese Hercules in the gardens designed by André Le Nôtre for Nicolas Fouquet at Vaux-le-Vicomte.
BELOW: The Thinker by Auguste Rodin in the Musée Rodin gardens.
OVERLEAF: View from couturier Martin Grant's window in the Marais.
ENDPAPER: Detail of *CraterCorten*, a sculpture by Arik Levy in Paris.